The postmodernist always rings twice

Reflections on culture in the 90s

Gilbert Adair

FOURTH ESTATE · *London*

First published in Great Britain in 1992 by
Fourth Estate Limited
289 Westbourne Grove
London W11 2QA

A catalogue record for this book is available from the British Library.

ISBN 1–85702–067–7

Typeset by York House Typographic Limited
Printed in Great Britain by Cambridge University Press

The publisher and author gratefully acknowledge the following, in which earlier versions of some of the essays in this book appeared: *The Guardian, The Sunday Correspondent, Esquire, The Times Literary Supplement, The Independent* and *The Sunday Times.*

for Clive Hirschhorn

Contents

The postmodernist always rings twice

'And don't you find it exhausting to go rushing about day after day?' 'Exhausting? Good Lord, no! It's great fun!' Volkov said happily. 'In the morning I read the papers – one must be au courant with everything, know the news. Thank heaven my job at the Civil Service doesn't require my presence at the office. All I'm supposed to do is to have dinner twice a week with the head of my department. Then I go visiting people I haven't seen for some time – well, then – er – there's always a new actress in the Russian or in the English theatre. The opera season will be opening soon and I shall book seats for it. And now I'm in love – summer is coming – Misha has been promised leave – we'll go for a month to their estate for a change. We can do some shooting there. They have splendid neighbours who give bals champêtres. Lydia and I will go for walks in the woods, go boating, pick flowers – Oh!' and he spun round and round with delight. 'However, I must be off. Good-bye,' he said, trying in vain to have a good look at himself in the dusty mirror.

Oblomov

Since this is a book whose protagonist is the first person singular, it's perhaps fitting that its prefatory essay begin with a personal anecdote. Several years ago, finding myself 'up for' the position of film critic on the *Washington Post*, I was faced with the immediate decision of whether or not to fly over to Washington for a preliminary interview (more at my own expense than the newspaper's, as I recollect). Actually, the whole job offer was the sort of initially gratifying windfall that I ended by regretting had ever tumbled into my lap, since I couldn't already help suspecting that, no matter the decision I did take, I would, at some time or other, at some level of my being or other, end by regretting that too. I certainly recall having, with an acquaintance who was also a film critic, a long argument over whether I truly wanted the post. My case against even applying for it was exclusively subjective: I knew not a soul in Washington, a city whose culture was in any event almost entirely political. My acquaintance counter-argued that the *Washington Post* was one of the most prestigious newspapers in the world (O Bernstein and Woodward! O Hoffman and Redford!) and that the city itself boasted an opera house, theatres, museums, galleries, cinemas, concert halls and lots and lots of good browsable bookstores. Don't forget (I felt like adding) the White House and the Lincoln Memorial.

For there was, I knew, a crucial flaw in the logic of his argument, on which, during the discussion itself, I couldn't quite put my finger. It was only much later that same night, one of several restless nights before I eventually declined the offer with thanks, that I cornered it. It was a flaw in what might be called the *sociology* of culture. Yes, naturally, as a capital city after all, Washington would be prolific in opera houses, theatres, museums, galleries, cinemas, concert halls and bookstores, but what, I said to myself, did these *venues* have to do with 'culture'? Not only were they not a solution to all the pother and ado of my resettlement, my sociocultural displacement – what? could I see myself, like Oblomov's busy friend Volkov, trotting off to the opera on Monday evening, the theatre on Tuesday, reading the new Nicholson Baker novel on Wednesday, taking in a gallery opening on Thursday, catching an art house revival of *Sunset Boulevard* on Friday and so on, week after week, month after month? – but they seemed to me to epitomise a lamentably dated, even obsolete conception of what culture is and how it functions (if culture may be said actively to 'function').

What my acquaintance appeared to be implying was that, for someone as well-read and well-informed as I flatter myself to be, someone to whom the exercise of aesthetic and intellectual discernment is both necessary and proper, the mere existence of such venues, and the opportunity they provided for the regular stimulation of that discernment, represented conclusive evidence of the city's cultural richness and resonance. If that *was* what he believed, he was already well behind the times. The idea of culture as something which has to be tracked down exclusively in galleries and opera houses, in theatres and bookstores, in cinemas and museums, has long been discredited. Alongside columns on the latest books, plays, films, concerts and exhibitions, every self-respecting newspaper in this country now routinely runs features on pop music, jazz, bestselling novels, television, design, advertising and the media in general, and only fogeyish diehards (who exist, heaven knows) still refuse to acknowledge these phenomena, be they proper 'art' or not, as part of what we currently think of as 'culture'. But I would go further. What I would seriously propose is that culture and art as we have come to comprehend them are so far from being synonymous or coextensive that they ought to be regarded as entities wholly distinct and discrete from one another; that culture, in effect, *begins where art ends and ends where art begins.*

Culture, like God and politics, is 'everywhere' – except, perhaps, in the work of art which has traditionally been considered its most direct and legitimate expression. The individual at home reading a novel by Anita Brookner, say, or in a theatre watching a play by Harold Pinter or in the Tate Gallery scrutinising one of Francis Bacon's screaming Popes is not at that precise instant having what I would define as a cultural experience. The work of art becomes a 'work of culture' only when it has been externalised, extrapolated from, thought about, talked about, read about, communicated and shared. Culture in this sense of the word is *applied* art, as one refers to applied mathematics. And the differences between the two concepts, at first paradoxical, become increasingly evident. Culture is extraverted; art is introverted. Culture is by very definition public and gregarious; art, even inside a gallery, a theatre or a cinema, is a private matter, a *tête-à-tête* encounter. (To create the desired intimacy in these venues the light is invariably filtered or dimmed or else switched off altogether.) Culture thrives on a continuous and pluralist discourse, a constant, febrile, impatient chatter; art demands silence from its public, silence and patience. Culture evolves (inevitably); art endures (or not).

What awaited me, then, in Washington, for all its fine theatres, museums, galleries, cinemas, concert halls and bookstores – what awaited me for the first several months at least of my sojourn there – was any number of private and (who knows?) profoundly soul-enhancing aesthetic experiences but virtually total exclusior from the city's true culture, which is, as I have said, political.

Perhaps the most appropriate analogy is, precisely, with a political campaign – that, for example, held for a general election. For the statutory twenty-one days we are subjected to the clamour of the election discourse, to its now completely mediatic culture – the rallies, photocalls, soundbites, press conferences, party political broadcasts and opinion polls. (Opinion polls constitute, rather, a meta-discourse, a discourse on the discourse, a self-reflexive commentary on what has already been said and thought elsewhere, and nowadays they generate in their turn a *meta*-meta-discourse, the so-called 'poll of polls': how very postmodern even electioneering has become!) Then election day dawns at what certainly seems like long last and we find ourselves alone inside a booth in a church hall. Everything, the discourse and the meta-discourse and the meta-meta-discourse, has narrowed to this neutral instant of pure formality, this pregnant present tense, in which all options but one are to be closed off. And if it is towards this instant that our entire political activity has appeared to be converging, it's worth reminding ourselves nevertheless that casting a vote, the supposed culmination and crux of the democratic process, is *something we do only twice in a decade*. During the long inactive years between elections, politics for virtually all of us means talking about politics, thinking about politics, reading about politics – *and nothing else*. It's not the pathetic act of voting once every five years that sustains our interest, such as it is, in the country's political life. On the contrary, it's that foregoing interest in the country's political life, a cultural, gregarious interest in personalities, speeches, scandals, leaked documents, cabinet reshuffles and of course, if often bringing up the rear, the famous 'issues', that eventually prompts us (some of us) to vote.

So it is currently, if on a quite different timescale, with the arts. In a sense, culture might be described as the permanent campaign by which the arts are promoted, except that our votes are being canvassed by not just three but hundreds of interested parties, novelists, dramatists, composers, painters, film directors, the vast majority of whom are fated to lose their deposit. Cultural literacy is therefore not a question of reading novels or poetry or going to theatres, cinemas, concert halls and museums, not a question of *casting votes*, which, again, most of us do only very rarely. It is founded, rather, on an informed awareness of what is to be seen at any given moment in these venues; on an alertness to the issues aired in the latest books and the debates, if any, that they have inspired; on a knowledge of how these works interconnect with each other and express, or not, the spirit of the times; on an acquaintance with which books and films and plays have won which prizes and how such prizes have reflected on both prizewinners and prizegivers. Prizes, festivals, magazine profiles, newspaper reviews, biographies, bestseller lists, questionnaires, publicised feuds, gala premières, suits for plagiarism, scandals, personal appearances, interviews, obituaries, anthologies, manifestos, readings, signing sessions, *Kaleidoscope* and the *Late Show*, the Groucho and the Garrick – *that*, representing wellnigh everything the purists despise (and not a few of those directly involved have been known in private to disparage) as fundamentally inimical to any true culture, *that* is the stuff of which contemporary culture is made.

Colette once said that it was unnecessary to read the great books as they gave off an aura. And to test that theory I quoted a brief passage from *Oblomov* at the head of this essay, convinced as I was that no one reading a book called *The Postmodernist Always Rings Twice*, even someone who had never read a word of Goncharov's novel, would fail to know who Oblomov was – whether, learnedly, as the personification of the 'redundant man' in nineteenth-century Russian literature or, more obscurely, as an aristocrat famous for never getting out of bed – and except, to be sure, for the pleasure of actually discovering Goncharov's (albeit slightly, subtly disappointing) classic, perhaps that's all one does need to know, given how much else is craning meanwhile to attract one's attention. In short, every culturally literate person, every *culturatus*, must know who Oblomov is, if he or she intends to participate in the cultural discourse, but no one will ever be blackballed from that discourse for not recognising the name 'Goncharov' or not having read his novel from cover to cover. It has given off, once and for all, its aura.

The very idea sounds preposterously philistine, yet we all know it to be the truth. Reading Goncharov's novel *Oblomov*, when there is so much else to read and see and hear, may give one an insight into the nineteenth-century Russian soul and conceivably the Russian soul *per se* (if such a thing exists), it may make one a 'better human being', it will certainly make one better-read, but it will not or not much better than fractionally make one a more culturally literate person. And in this, an era when the increasingly tentacular media are now equipped to pipe these auras into every household equipped to receive them, the statement no longer applies exclusively to great books but to almost every book as well as to every play, film, opera and exhibition.

We culturati find ourselves peppered, on a practically daily basis, by the injunctions of deliriously excitable critics. 'Not to be missed!' they shriek at us. Or 'Beg, buy, borrow or steal a ticket!' Or else 'If you read only one new novel this year, let it be [say] *Time's Arrow*!' We register the precise temperature of this enthusiasm; we calmly, perhaps only half-consciously, assimilate its implications; and just as calmly, even just as half-consciously, we proceed to miss what wasn't on any account to be missed. We don't beg, borrow, steal or in ninety-nine cases out of a hundred even buy a ticket. As everyone knows, as the critics themselves know (and, of course, I'm quite well aware that the sort of codified enthusiasm I've been parodying is little more than handily citable rhetoric, not designed to be read as a literal command to be obeyed), the vast majority of their regular readers miss the vast majority of novels, plays, films, operas, concerts and exhibitions that have been recommended to them. It may not be, whatever Colette says, exactly 'unnecessary' to read the great books. (We may after all read anything we like; equally, though, and putting it rather paradoxically, we may dislike anything we like.) But to be culturally literate today means above all being capable of making meaningful and productive connections within the contemporary history of art and ideas; possessing a genuine comprehension of that history as a constantly evolving continuum of intellectual and ideological currents; and, to apply a bright new gloss to a whiskery old gag, not necessarily reading all the books but reading all the reviews.

In an article published in *Travels in Hyperreality* Umberto Eco already made much the same point in relation to what he referred to as 'sports chatter':

> Present-day sports, then, is essentially a discussion of the sports press. At several removes there remains the actual sport, which might as well not even exist. If through some diabolical machination of the Mexican government and chairman Avery Brundage, in agreement with all the TV networks in the world, the Olympics were not to take place, but were narrated daily and hourly through fictitious images, nothing in the international sports system would change, nor would the sports discutants feel cheated. So sport as practice, as activity, no longer exists, or exists for economic reasons (for it is easier to make an athlete run than to invent a film with actors who pretend to run); and there exists only chatter about chatter about sport.

In the same way, the arts in this country exist *principally to fuel the culture industry*, to furnish the gregarity of the cultural discourse with a constantly replenished and potentially inexhaustible supply of referents. To adapt Eco's droll conspiracy fantasy – it would make not an iota of difference to the majority of people in this country, even those who consider themselves culturally informed, if the plays, films, books, operas, concerts and exhibitions that they have been ordered to see were totally chimerical entities, pure fictions collectively perpetrated by those whose profession or vocation it is to keep the culture industry oiled and operative.

The fact is that most people read reviews less to know what they should be seeing than to know what other people are seeing. For every brave individual who actually decides to see a play by Howard Brenton or read a novel by Penelope Lively or visit an exhibition of Henry Moore's sculpture, there are a thousand whose familiarity with it, a familiarity sufficient for their purposes, has derived exclusively from the media-piped aura that it gives off. They are liable to be sneered at as mere 'readers of reviews', yet they are, after all, most of us most of the time.

Culture is a multifarious moment in the history of a society, a self-propagating, self-perpetuating grid of interconnections, an infinitely extensible field of free associations. Take just one example from among countless: the book by Martin Amis already cited. What confronts the reader of *Time's Arrow* is a short novel, brilliant and arguably specious, about a German surgeon performing unimaginable pseudo-medical experiments inside a concentration camp before absconding to the United States under an assumed identity. And what of course differentiates it from the ruck of contemporary fiction is that its narrative unfolds in reverse, anti-chronological order. Beyond that reading, however, or prior to it, or without its ever having taken place, there exists for the culturatus an alternative way in which such a novel may be 'read'. Less from the text itself (which, as all recent critical methodologies concur, requires no external biographical data as a support to comprehension) than from its status as a significant artefact of the cultural moment, of what the French call *l'air du temps* and what the British call the *zeitgeist*, there radiates a series of avenues of pursuit and speculation which will enrich his reading of *Time's Arrow* not as art but as culture, not as a text but as an *event*.

One such avenue would radiate from the identity of the author himself and encompass *en route* his standing as *the* novelist of his generation, his poutily brattish good looks, his apparently chronic (and possibly unjust) inability to win the Booker Prize, his no less celebrated father, etc. Each of these would then generate tributary avenues, some of them thoroughfares, not a few of them impasses. From an inventory that makes no claim to exhaustivity we might cite the comparative status of Amis's close rivals, Barnes, McEwan, Ackroyd and company; the influence on his work of the American vernacular style; Kingsley Amis's own career, his reactionary views and general 'Old Devil' blimpishness; the history of the Booker Prize and its relation to the Goncourt; etc. Another avenue would proceed from the novel's organising principle of an inverted narrative. Is this merely a gimmick ('I haven't read the book but I peeked at the first page to see how it comes out!') or, as Sarah Dunant proposed on *The Late Show*, does it permit us to see the Holocaust in a completely new light? and what on earth did she mean by that? that the Holocaust has gone *stale*? and indeed shouldn't there be a moratorium (awkward choice of word in the circumstances) on all fictional representations of the concentration camps? and isn't it frankly sexist of *Private Eye* to refer to Sarah Dunant as 'Brains' or is it acceptable because she actually does resemble such a character in *Thunderbirds*? and surely the whole issue of political correctness. . . and. . . and. . . and. . . and. . .

That may seem like a defence of the so-called chattering classes (yet, after all, why not? The origin of the expression 'chattering classes' is traceable to the most ignorant of cultural demonologies; the word 'chattering' is pure cant; and in every exaltation of action over speech there will always reside a covert threat of terrorism), but it is exactly how the discourse of our contemporary culture functions and, as can be seen, its fundamental articulation is one of gregarity, of conversation. Naturally, it's possible, even laudable, to wish to close one's ears to all that 'noise', as Salman Rushdie once described it, but that noise *is* the hum of cultural gregarity – what a French historian, Marc Fumaroli, called *la rap culture*.

Salman Rushdie, precisely. If the garrulous buzz routinely set off by a new book by Amis or Barnes or Ackroyd feels uncomfortably close to mere gossip (but, again, why not? Gossip is surely as essential to the welfare of the human psyche as play, and it constitutes the basic 'culture' of an office, a factory or any place of work), consider instead what is unquestionably the most important cultural event of our time: the affair of *The Satanic Verses*.

Now, it's understandable that Rushdie himself should repeatedly plead that his adversaries return to the text of the novel itself before passing judgment (in a uniquely unfigurative sense) on both it and him. To Sara Rance in the *Observer* he remarked, 'I don't think it unusual for a book to be judged without being read, but it hasn't happened on quite this scale before. What I never expected was for the book to be so absolutely drowned in the noise. People came to the conclusion that they didn't actually need to read it to have their opinions.' He's right. I myself (belatedly) read *The Satanic Verses* because of my irritation at hearing it dismissed as unreadable by acquaintances who, when questioned, would admit quite unabashedly that they hadn't actually read it. There can be no equivocation here: to *judge The Satanic Verses*, or any work of literature for that matter, one must have read it.

Culture, however, in the sense in which I've been using the term, is only marginally concerned with judgments. If the novel itself is still, naturally, a crucial element in the discourse surrounding the Rushdie affair, it's neither the exclusive nor by now, alas, the most significant element. The issues that its publication has raised – the inviolability of any individual's right to freedom of speech and opinion, the laws of blasphemy in this country as they apply to religious minorities, the hypocrisy of the current British government vis-à-vis that of Iran, the wisdom or unwisdom of publishing a paperback edition in the wake of the *fatwa* – are answerable only by a reading, not of *The Satanic Verses*, but of the countless articles which have been written, the statements issued, the debates held, since the scandal erupted in 1989. Not even an understanding of what precisely it was in the novel that inflamed fundamentalist Muslims can be culled (by the Western, non-Islamic reader) from internal evidence alone, unless one is also prepared to read the Koran and related sacred texts. There, too, it is via so-called secondary or 'cultural' readings that information and thus comprehension are to be gained.

This is in no sense to diminish the horror and injustice of Rushdie's own plight or to imply that *The Satanic Verses* was a kind of monstrous McGuffin, engendering a debate from which it itself, in the subsequent brouhaha of the affair, became queerly detachable – only that the novel has been 'culturised' into an event.

What it is, then, that transforms artists or 'personalities' into the media's coddled or manhandled darlings is their value as agents and repositories of cultural debate. For there are inevitably 'good' and 'bad' conductors of cultural currents, whatever their respective achievements in solely artistic terms. Nigel Kennedy, for example. Certainly since adopting his oikish 'Nige' guise, Kennedy has become one of the 'good' conductors. The basis of the polemic that still rages around his person, pitting music lovers against those 'who don't know much about music but know what they like', is elementary enough. To wit: Is he a good thing or a bad thing for classical music, a good thing for having introduced the timeless symmetries and serenities of Brahms and Vivaldi to those who would otherwise never have encountered them or a bad thing for having connived at drowning out not only the quality of his playing but the quality of the music played by the 'noise' surrounding his own gaudy public image? Beyond the immediate premises of the controversy, though, it's possible to argue that Kennedy is a good thing precisely because he caused the question to be posed in the first place, because he has succeeded, with the release of each of his records, in provoking a debate on just what and who classical music is for. In short, he sends out far more *signals* than virtually any other musician of his age, talent and experience, signals relating to the politics of high and low culture, to productions of *Carmen* and

Aïda in sports arenas, to the forays of Kiri Te Kanawa and Placido Domingo into operetta and musical comedy, to the spectacle of Pavarotti in Hyde Park and the selection of 'Nessun Dorma' as the World Cup's theme tune, to the legitimacy or not of staging *Pacific Overtures* at the English National Opera and *Guys and Dolls* at the National Theatre.

If Nigel Kennedy is significant it's because, for better or worse, he *generates significance*, he produces meanings, he has had, by the affront of nothing much more than his personality, the effect of calling a number of pious and entrenched cultural prejudices into question. The debates held in his name are not 'more' or 'less' enriching than the music itself (even to entertain such a comparison would be absurd), but they *are* enriching nevertheless.

Nor need the only good conductor of cultural speculation be some individual personality, some brilliant cynosure, some 'star'. It can just as well be a book (*The Runaway Soul*) or a film (*Basic Instinct*), a tribute (the knighting of Ian McKellen) or a scandal (the quarrel over Jacques Derrida's honorary degree from Cambridge), an institution (the Arts Council) or a debate (the recent polemic, for example, on the respective virtues of elitist and populist culture as represented in the red corner by John Keats and in the blue corner by Bob Dylan).

Thus debates are debated, discussions are discussed and questions are questioned. There is a fittingly *postmodernist* self-referentiality to the cultural discourse as it now functions in this country – fitting precisely because our culture is at present traversing the post-modern moment of its social history. Few 'isms', however, have provoked as much perplexity and suspicion as postmodernism, no doubt because of the way in which that already contentious word 'modern' is sandwiched between a prefix and a suffix, each as dubious as the other. What, then, in the light of the numerous theories, models and interpretations which have accrued to the term since it first surfaced in the early seventies, does that moment actually imply?

One can find a witty allegory of postmodernism in *Reflections on 'The Name of the Rose'*, the limpid little volume written by Umberto Eco to explain the genesis of his bestselling novel. He defines the postmodernist's attitude as 'that of a man who loves a very cultivated woman and knows he cannot say to her, "I love you madly", because he knows that she knows (and that she knows that he knows) that these words have already been written by Barbara Cartland. Still,' continues Eco, 'there is a solution. He can say, "As Barbara Cartland would put it, I love you madly." At this point, having avoided false innocence, having said clearly that it is no longer possible to speak innocently, he will nevertheless have said what he wanted to say to the woman: that he loves her, but that he loves her in an age of lost innocence. If the woman goes along with this, she will have received a declaration of love all the same.'

As that characteristic specimen of Eco-logy bears out, quotation is very much the name of the postmodernist rose. Yet, for the layman, hoping to understand not just the cultural but the political and social implications of postmodernism, and recoiling from the often rebarbative brilliance of Jean Baudrillard, still the movement's most fashionable theorist (one major problem with Baudrillard is that his own prose is a self-reflexive symptom of what it is concerned to analyse – which is to say, he writes 'postmodernistically', whereas André Breton, for example, never wrote about Surrealism 'surrealistically'), there are two basic questions to be asked. One, how can anything, except perhaps in the context of science-fiction, be 'post' modernity, when modernity surely is 'now'? Two, if one is capable of recognising E. L. Doctorow's *Ragtime* as a postmodern novel, Tim Burton's *Batman* as a postmodern film and Richard Rogers's Thames-side Lloyds building as an example of postmodern architecture, what can three so dissimilar works conceivably have in common?

The first point to be grasped (an insultingly evident one for many readers) is that 'modern' refers not to a temporal continuum but to an *aesthetic* – that, precisely, of the Modern Movement, which flowed throughout the first half of the century and started to ebb in the immediate postwar years. Thus the existence of postmodernism was contingent on the extinction of modernism proper, and its advent was related, in the analysis of its most eminent American theorist, Fredric Jameson, to a parallel evolution in international capitalism, from market capitalism through the 'monopoly stage' to our own postindustrialist or multinational era, the era in the West of the so-called service industries and rampant commodification. It's hardly by chance, as Jameson notes, that the most conspicuous of postmodern buildings are hotels.

As the Modern Movement sputtered out in a series of increasingly marginalised spasms of avant-gardism, as at the same time it could no longer credibly feign resistance to a culturo-commercial mainstream in which it was constantly subsumed (Van Gogh had to wait until after his death to be recognised, Julian Schnabel until after his first one-man show), what was sought was an escape route out of the impasse. And this was found in a knowing retrieval of the past, in which artists would square the circle by both parodying and revivifying the strategies of an earlier generation, making these strategies operative a second time around (the postmodernist always rings twice, as you might say) by inserting them within ironic, if not entirely ironic, quotation marks. The Wildean credo of the postmodernist might be that each man parodies the thing he loves.

Ragtime therefore interpolates, in the episode of its black protagonist Coalhouse, a (serious) parody of the Kleist novella *Michael Kohlhaas*, and throughout his narrative Doctorow combines historical with purely fictional characters. So did Walter Scott, to be sure, but Doctorow calls the reader's attention to the procedure in so overt a fashion that it too seems to be parodying the traditional historical novel. On a more mercenary, less 'noble' level (for although it has been claimed of postmodernism that it dissolves a number of immemorial hierarchies, these tend to sneak in through the back door), the merchandising mania attending the release of a blockbuster like *Batman*, the franchised sales of toys, masks and teeshirts, is somehow inscribed within the textures and trappings of the movie itself. Art forms which would once have cancelled each other out (comic strips, German Expressionist films, the paintings of Edward Hopper) now harmoniously coexist, no longer made available to a handful of initiates as covert influences on the director but flagrantly paraded for all to see, 'merchandised' as so many cultural brand names (to begin with the Batman logo itself) that the spectator is expected to recognise and take pleasure in recognising. As for Rogers's Lloyd's building, its architecture differs from the rigorous and puritanical modernism of a Le Corbusier, say, in its unashamed eagerness to embrace rather than reject the glitzy yuppie euphoria that generated its existence in the first place.

That is what Jameson meant by 'the logic of late capitalism' (the title of his most influential essay on the subject) and what Eco meant by the end of 'an age of innocence'. Postmodernism is, almost by definition, a transitional cusp of social, cultural, economic and ideological history when modernism's earnest principles and preoccupations have ceased to function but have not yet been replaced by a totally new system of values. It represents a moment of suspension before the batteries are recharged for the new millennium, an acknowledgment that preceding the future is a strange and hybrid interregnum that might be called *the last gasp of the past*.

It is a moment, clearly, saturated in historical awareness; and for all its froth of brainy playfulness, of intellectual fooling and pretending, it has been accompanied by a wave of wholly serious, scholary developments in our attitude towards the art of the past. (This is a facet of the postmodern which has gone quite unnoticed, even by Eco and Baudrillard.) *Item*, the fact that 'early' music is now increasingly played on the authentic instruments of its period and not, as formerly was the case, on anachronistic pianos, organs and violins. *Item*, that recording companies have begun painstakingly to explore the most marginal and even eccentric byways of musical history. *Item*, that, in a kindred spirit, music festivals around the world are starting to revive, for the first time in many decades, even sometimes centuries, long-neglected works by minor *bel canto* or *verismo* composers; or première little-known operas by Pfitzner, Schreker, Weill, Korngold, etc. *Item*, that it has become virtually unimaginable for the National Theatre or the Royal Shakespeare Company to abridge, re-edit or otherwise tamper with, save directorially, the Bard (or, for that matter, many a lesser ornament of our theatrical heritage). *Item*, that there has been, in recent years, been a veritable rash of literary reissues, primarily from the teens, twenties and thirties of this century. *Item*, that scholars are currently vying with one another to establish ever more authentic editions of classic texts, and that Joyce, Orwell and Lawrence among others have (not always happily) enjoyed the posthumous privilege of having their most celebrated novels republished free of the printing errors and censorious attentions which marred their original editions. *Item*, that even minor, academic painters of the nineteenth century and earlier have been accorded definitive one-man shows in the nation's museums; ditto for book illustrators, political cartoonists and portrait photographers. *Item*, that in the cinema low-budget European 'art films', emancipated from all but the humblest economic pressures (since not even their producers expect to profit by them), have been granted the licence to explore a radical and often extraordinarily productive avant-gardism (e.g. Straub, Godard, Ruiz), thereby aligning themselves at last with the experimental front in music and literature and painting. *Item*, that a number of once mutilated films (*A Star Is Born, New York, New York, Heaven's Gate* and of course, the granddaddy of them all, Abel Gance's sixty-year-old *Napoléon*) have been widely re-released in intact prints. *Item*, that encompassing all of the above, there has existed for several years now a mania for 'complete works' of every category and description: the symphonies of Shostakovich and even Glazunov issued in single box sets; the belated appearance of hitherto unpublished texts by writers as diverse as Kipling and Salinger; the publication of the deleted chapter ('The Wasp in a Wig') of *Through the Looking-Glass* and of Shakespeare's supposed 'lost' poems and plays. And so on, and on.

Although it would perhaps be premature to interpret these data as the collectively willed expression of a generalised condition, there does seem to be little doubt that our consideration of the literary and artistic achievements of the past has of late been infused by a movement (more precisely, a conflux of convergent movements) towards a culminative sense of authenticity, a fullness of informed appreciation, a comprehensive overview of accomplishment, towards what might be called a cult of cultural integrality. This age of ours, an age of retrenchment rather than experiment, of consumerist as much as creative stocktaking, has tended to stretch all its available resources, its already established co-ordinates, practically to bursting point, instead of opening up new formal parameters by which our reading of the world might be redefined and reanimated.

But these are, to be sure, only two of the more high-minded faces, the innovatory and the archival, of the whole complex postmodern phenomenon. Concurrent with them there has also been an exploitation, unwitting or only half-witting for the most part, of its sociology and sensibility, and it is undoubtedly this reduction of postmodernism to a mere glossy, superficial, mannerist coating of style which has tended to bring the term into disrepute.

In the haemorrhage of images typical of contemporary culture the past (mostly the recent past) has been transformed into a mammoth lucky dip. All you have to do, if you are a maker of TV commercials or pop promos, a designer of shop windows or record sleeves, the editor of *The Face* or *GQ*, an architect, a painter, even a marketing entrepreneur, is plunge in and scoop out whatever happens to address your particular need. With the decades mingling indiscriminately (the 'recent past' is that which is divisible by decades, not centuries), nothing, *absolutely nothing*, will, any can longer need seem dated or outmoded. Rare is the artistic expression of the earlier years of this century that has not been artificially regilded or else pulverised into a thousand glinting particles by the inflationary, insatiable image-spinning of the present. It may be no more serious than the reprise of advertising motifs and logos that had previously been dropped because of undesirably passé connotations – the Bisto Kids and the Metro-Goldwyn-Mayer lion, both lately restored to their full, prewar, glowingly kitsch splendour. Or it may be the injection of a shrill populism into a form as allegedly élitist as opera – as in the case of *Aria*, a recent portmanteau film made up of individually selected numbers from a dozen operas, each visualised by a different director (Godard, Altman, Jarman, etc.). What did it matter that any given episode bore much the same relationship to the masterpiece from which it was extracted as a wine gum bears to a bottle of vintage Châteauneuf-du-Pape? What did it matter that all those tedious choruses and recitatives ended up on the cutting-room floor? The pseudo-postmodern point was that, by being fragmented in this way, a handful of long and 'boring' operas had been magically metamorphosed into short, snappy opera promos.

On occasion such pawing over the past attains a truly macabre dimension. A few years ago, as though to demonstrate how new wine would taste better if poured into an old bottle, Porsche 're-released' the nineteen-fifties Speedster model whose principal claim to notoriety happened to be that it was the automobile in which James Dean killed himself. There the paradox was not merely that, once more, nothing had been made to appear quite so up-to-the-minute as the past but that what the Speedster's new generation of purchasers were getting for their money was a car that had been authenticated, as it were, by a fatal accident.

So one could continue. From those dreamy Edward Hopper-esque bistros, neither wholly American nor wholly 'Continental', neither wholly of the past nor wholly of the present, which play so predominant a role in the advertising of soft drinks and alcohol-free lagers, to the enduring taste for a 'Laura Ashley' school of fabrics and furnishings which, not content simply to mass-market a style whose very cachet was once that it could not be industrialised, also contrives to effect an instantaneously faded quality that further serves to camouflage the manufacturing process, from the sudden fad for Forster adaptations in the cinema to the endless musical comedy revivals that have come to monopolise the stages of the West End, from the tabloid depiction of the Royal Family's quotidian round as just another soap opera (or, to be more precise, Ivor Novello-ish soap operetta) to the ruthlessly systematic appropriation by book jacket designers of a pallidly Impressionist school of British painters (in the Tate Gallery I once heard a woman remark to her companion, as they squinted at a murkily gaslit Sickert: 'That would make an awfully nice Virago cover, don't you think?'), the postmodern phenomenon has gradually infiltrated every vacant pocket of our lives and lifestyles.

Thus, at this juncture of our cultural history, assailed as we are by a blitz of often conflicting and contradictory signals from the communications media, we find ourselves at the centre of what Baudrillard has termed a 'universe of persuasion'. And to make sense of the increasingly bewildering diversity of messages received, it is clearly no longer sufficient, even if we were possessed of the necessary, inclination, will and energy, merely to strive to see as many plays, films, operas and exhibitions as humanly possible – in other words, to catch what the critics tell us mustn't be missed.

To be sure, there is likely always to exist the ornery kind of eccentric who is prepared to brave the elements (which these days tend to be not so much natural as urban) in order to take in a play, concert or exhibition instead of just soaking up its reflected glory from his TV set like a low-income swinger tanning himself in front of a sun lamp; prepared to venture forth in whatever climate (economic as well as meteorological) to be vouchsafed something *live*, some precious, throbbing fragment of life, be it live actors, live musicians or 'live' paintings. And there is always likely to exist the kind of film buff purist for whom nothing will ever diminish the cachet of the single trump card with which the cinema is capable of defeating television – a bigger screen (even if that would seem to be making a manly, not to say macho, virtue out of size itself); for whom it remains essential to the experience of watching a film that the screen engulf him and focalise all his mental and ocular faculties.

Yet one already begins to feel that there is something strangely archaic about arriving at a theatre, an opera house or a cinema at a prespecified hour, taking one's prespecified place in the auditorium and subjecting oneself to a prespecified work of art or entertainment circumscribed by its own prespecified rhythm and running time. The truly postmodern attitude to culture, by contrast, will emphasise the exercise of free choice, free circulation and free connection-making, all intellectual freedoms precluded or at the very least cramped and contained by the need of the more traditional art forms and venues to fascinate, to hypnotise, to *cast a collective spell*.

In the postmodern world the notion of culture as something exclusively located in a specialised venue will be, as I have suggested, no longer operable; culture will increasingly come to us and not vice versa. It will no longer be a question of congregation but of circulation, no longer of venues but of avenues. And theatres, cinemas, concert halls and museums are destined to be marginalised (if it hasn't yet happened) as the anachronistic relics, the very last, secularised and frequently trivialised gasp, of the sacred and ritualistic in a cultural context.

It was of course Walter Benjamin, in his celebrated essay on the revolution wrought by the advent of photography on the mediated representation of the world, *The Work of Art in the Age of Mechanical Reproduction*, a seminal text if ever there was, who was the first to register the seismic shift that that revolution had effected in our understanding of what a work of art was and how it functioned. In it he wrote, notably, that:

An analysis of art in the age of mechanical reproduction must do justice to these relationships [between 'authentic' works of art with their basis in ritual and those works subsequent to 'the rise of the first truly revolutionary means of reproduction, photography'] for they lead us to an all-important insight: for the first time in world history, mechanical reproduction emancipates the work of art from its parasitical dependence on ritual. To an ever greater degree the work of art reproduced becomes the work of art designed for reproducibility. From a photographic negative, for example, one can make any number of prints; to ask for the 'authentic' print makes no sense. But the instant the criterion of authenticity ceases to be applicable to artistic productions, the total function of art is reversed.

This question of the 'original', whose presence was, for Benjamin, 'the prerequisite to the concept of authenticity', is central to the prophetic importance of his essay. 'Originality', in the historicist sense in which he employs the word, has become the luxury, the exclusive preserve, the private hunting ground, of state and corporate institutions and of a conspicuous but nevertheless tiny cluster of millionaire collectors: the 'originals' of the very greatest paintings do not even travel abroad any longer because of the increasingly prohibitive cost of insuring them. As far as the Old Masters are concerned (and the New Masters are catching up amazingly fast), we have become so familiarised with the reproduced image, in albums, monographs, catalogues, biographies and even Sunday supplement spreads, that the (for most of us infrequent) experience of actually strolling around a museum has become invested with a curiously antiquarian quality, a sense of rehearsing a faintly dated, almost 'period' ritual. These 'live' (or dead?) paintings at which we dutifully gaze have that unmediated rawness of a woman's naked legs that strikes the eye accustomed rather to seeing them sheathed in silk stockings. In addition, fewer and fewer visitors to the institutional caverns and canyons of culture find that they can adequately function without the assistance of an earphone commentary – without, in other words, the accompaniment of *la rap culture* – and it's by no means a foregone conclusion that it's by the visual rather than the aural message that they will made more culturally literate.

Since Benjamin published his essay in 1936, moreover, the means of mechanical reproduction have become vertiginously diversified: the questions that it raises can no longer be confined to painting and photography. If, in his own words, 'for the first time in the process of pictorial reproduction, photography freed the hand of the most important artistic functions which henceforth devolved only upon the eye looking into the lens' (which explains the predominance, in both their numbers and their relative skills, of amateur photographers over dilettantes in any other artistic sphere), then related liberties can henceforth be taken with virtually all of the arts.

The basic concept here, paradoxically enough, is that of 'reading'. Reading not merely in the semiotician's sense of 'interpreting', 'deciphering' and 'decoding', but in the sense of *programming*; the sense in which such an approach to culture implies the wilful fragmentation of attention and study, the regular disruption, dislocation and interrogation of continuity and flow, the casual subjection of the work of art to one's own natural or domestic rhythms, often in a near-total indifference to those imagined or intended by the artist. This is after all how we have always read books themselves. Not since the existence of illuminated manuscripts in the Middle Ages has the Book – which in my earlier collection of essays, *Myths & Memories*, I defined as 'the staple of the intelligence' – been influenced by the mystique of the original and the authentic. A book is a book. To say that books are mass-produced is to say absolutely nothing pejorative about them. (The sole remnant of the sacred in this field resides in the collection of rare first editions, and collectors of these are often notoriously insensitive to the quality of the texts that the books themselves enfold.) No one, save perhaps one of those millionaire collectors, has ever thought of a book as a 'reproduction' of the writer's original manuscript. And increasingly, with growing skill and confidence, that section of the public which regards itself as culturally informed is learning to 'read' all the arts as it reads books, exercising its freedom of choice and circulation so thoroughly and adroitly that the distinction between 'originals' and 'reproductions' is being rendered ever more meaningless.

Certainly, the retrieval and authentification of the cultural heritage that I mention above (the emended *Ulysses*, the reconstructed *Napoléon*, etc.) have been made possible by an ideology of reproduction that it would be hard to view as other than entirely beneficial, even if the results are not invariably satisfactory. But the principle is equally applicable to our relationship with current artworks.

Video recorders, for example, allow us to watch movies exactly as we have always read books. We interrupt them to answer the telephone or make ourselves coffee (and after such an interruption we tend to reactivate the tape a few frames back, just as we generally pick up a book a few pages prior to where we left it off). We may play back an especially affecting scene or freeze the frame on an especially beautiful (and, why not, erotic) image. If a gangster in a thriller, say, claims that he was not carrying a gun during a heist, we can actually, as with a book, revert to the scene (in both senses of the word) of the crime in order to verify whether or not he is telling the truth. We are no longer compelled to submit to the jurisdiction of an authoritarian author (or *auteur*), and it's quite possible, even likely, that movies of the future will be conceived and shot with just this kind of 'reading' in mind.

The compact disc recorder accords us similar freedoms where music and opera are concerned, allowing us to program the order in which we choose to listen to the various recorded numbers and even offering the bonus of a random selection key to preserve, if we wish, a capricious element of surprise. And, as though to compensate for the loss of the 'live' experience, a loss liable to be felt only by that fairly insignificant proportion of the community of music lovers who are regular rather than occasional opera- and concertgoers, the current recorded repertoire is infinitely more bountiful than any single public venue, no matter how prestigious, can afford to be, in both the range of the musical works on offer and the choice of the performers to which it has, and grants us, access. Recordings could even be said to constitute a more generous and indulgent form of *posterity*. How many operas, condemned to apparently definitive neglect by their notorious inability to 'hold the stage', have been posthumously salvaged from archival purgatory by some small and enterprising recording company?

Finally, there may even come a time when a painting in a museum will bear the same relation to the reproduced image of that painting that a manuscript bears to a published book. It will be regarded as a totem, a fetish, a curiosity, an artefact worth owning for its individual rarity and beauty but, if in itself 'finished' (as a writer's manuscript is after all finished), somehow not 'complete', bereft of that seamless surface gloss by which we now recognise and identify completeness, bereft of that reproductive sheen that is the only species of *patina* to which we any longer respond.

The principal consequence of this reproductive boom is what one might call (to employ a particularly unsightly neologism) an 'Oblomovisation' of culture. Like Oblomov, who refused to quit his bed to inspect the new Russian or English actress but who, it ultimately transpired, was as aware of everything that was 'going on' as though he had been tirelessly haring about town, the less culture we trouble ourselves to track down, the more culture we seem to have access to. Culture, in short, is something which 'happens' to us increasingly at home – in, as they say, our own space – and correspondingly less in those venues that were erected, mostly decades and even centuries ago, in its name.

And its principal victim is of course the theatre, which, by very definition, does not easily lend itself to any of the codified processes of reproduction. That the British theatre is in decline, in precipitous, perhaps terminal decline, can no longer be in doubt. The many and various symptoms speak for themselves: the defection of its professionals (not only performers but writers and directors) to film and television; the impoverishment of its repertoire; the steadily declining numbers of its devotees (and in the case of London's West End its unhealthy dependence on the seasonal tourist trade, the fatal sign of a cultural death rattle); the disaffection of younger audiences; above all, perhaps, the poverty and inbreeding of its mythocultural discourse. (Is Kenneth Branagh *the* Hamlet of his generation? Will Antony Sher's Richard III ever make us forget Olivier's? Are *these* Three Sisters better than *those* Three Sisters? For too much of the time the theatre would appear to be *talking to itself*.) And yet. This obstinate resistance to the age of mechanical reproduction may in the end be the theatre's salvation (always assuming that it still has the capacity to reinvent itself). It may precisely be what guarantees it, the most ancient of all the performing arts, an enduring role in a culture for which the *live*, the unrepeatable fragment of life, will continue to represent a primitive but possibly still potent signifier of the sacred.

This book, a collection of journalistic columns written over the past three years for a variety of publications, constitutes one individual's endeavours to make sense of, and meaning out of, the contemporary culture of this country, high and low alike, upmarket and down. It is, if you will, both the calendar of a period and a meta-discourse on its cultural discourse: what concerns me in these sixty brief essays is not, as is usually claimed of maverick cultural commentators like myself, the interstices of culture but rather the currents that flow between its multiple terminals. My methodology, if I may be said to possess one, has been to approach culture not directly but obliquely, with exactly the movement of the knight in chess – one step forward, two to the side, two steps forward, one to the side (fully exploiting, too, the knight's unique advantage of being able to leap over intermediate squares on the board).

It's a methodology that is frankly, if rather loosely, based on that pioneered during the fifties by Roland Barthes when he wrote, for a French weekly journal, the articles eventually collected in book form as *Mythologies*, and developed during the sixties, seventies and eighties by Umberto Eco when he wrote his not dissimilar essays for a Milanese daily and subsequently collected them in

Travels in Hyperreality. Although neither Barthes nor Eco was of course primarily a journalist, their dual example has revolutionised journalistic practices and conventions throughout Europe.

The interest of their work, however, resides not just in their methodology but in the fact that intellectuals were at last turning their attention to what had previously been regarded as the trivial connective tissue of culture – often, too, culture in its most populist forms. But therein lies the danger. Precisely because of their prior example, Barthes and Eco (and one should perhaps add Baudrillard) have made it increasingly difficult to write intelligently on the subject. Not because their undoubted erudition, acuity and (not least) charm have pre-empted everything we, their successors, might have to say on the matter (culture is evolving at too breakneck a speed for that to happen) but because we are not alone in having read Barthes and Eco, not alone in having assimilated their insights. Filmmakers, photographers, video promo directors, copywriters, the designers of record sleeves and typefaces have also read them, and they are far cleverer, certainly far cannier, than the self-styled semiologists who flatter themselves that they are 'decoding' their products.

Decoding? What is the point of decoding artefacts whose 'codes' were actually designed to be cracked, like those phoney communiqués that were fed to the German Intelligence Service during the Second World War? Why expend energy unearthing the potentially cultish properties of a technological novelty when its cultishness has been deliberately programmed into it by its sly devisers? Why endeavour to demystify the 'subtext' of a lager commercial when that supposed subtext could scarcely lie closer to the surface and is being forced on one's attention the way a card-sharper forces a card?

It's quite possible, for example, that the initially sluggish progress of satellite television derived in part from the considerably less than state-of-the-art feel of its dishes. Who wants to have one of these metallic cloth caps clamped to the side of their house, positively reeking of a proletariat culture of tabloid newspapers and darts championships? No matter how poor the satellite programming, if the satellite dishes had been as glossy and futuristic as compact discs, say, then they might have caught on as rapidly as, well, compact discs themselves.

CDs are, in fact, a notable case of preprogrammed cultishness. Who can resist these mercurially silvery little disks with just a hint of credit card iridescence to reinforce the enigma inherent in all records – that, until they are played, their mysterious surface autism offers no clue as to what they might contain? Who can resist that surplus value of necessary superfluousness (without futility there can be no real sense of luxury) represented by the random key that allows you to play tracks in any order you like? Why, even the little perspex boxes, snapping open and shut with the chic click of a silver cigarette case, have been designed for maximum tactile *jouissance*.

Now, it would be nice to imagine that the reader, having ingested the above, is musing 'Oh, I never thought of that' – which is, after all, the response elicited by all cultural commentators. But I confess to having few illusions that I might have taught anything at all to the individual or individuals responsible for the original design, since that design was probably the nitty-gritty of the whole exercise, the nub of the marketing operation.

If this book, then, is devoted to what I've called the discourse of contemporary British culture, it's obliged to recognise that none of the emblematic artifices and artefacts of that culture, be they movies, commercials, headlines, photographs, typefaces, fashions or fads, can any longer be trusted to be 'innocent'; that even if, let's say, the crisp elegance of the typeface in which this very essay is embedded emits a 'meaning' as much as does the text itself, that meaning is also just as conscious and deliberate. 'The medium is the message,' said Marshall McLuhan when he wanted to demonstrate how suspect the message was. What we must now acknowledge is that the medium itself is no less suspect.

Batman

Here it is at last, the distinguished thing, as, circumlocutory to his dying breath, Henry James is reported to have said an instant before expiring. The distinguished thing I refer to, though, is not death but the caped, hooded and wraithlike silhouette which has been hovering over the whole country for the last six weeks or so, death's dark, insidious agent and angel – in a word, *Batman*. This week, at last, the work in question arrives at the juncture of its public career when what was heretofore nothing but a rumour, a project, a poster and above all a graphic motif is transformed overnight into a film one can actually go and see; when the quasi-mythical object of innumerable fantasies actually comes to 'share one's own space'. And, at least for the potential spectator, it is this juncture which constitutes the film's very highest point of visibility, the apotheosis of all the marketing hyperbole, the instant at which the legend (of the film itself, not its protagonist) can be savoured in its full plenitude and promise. Poised to open nationwide, *Batman* will never again seem so desirable. For, once that potential spectator finds himself seated in the cinema, it will already have shrunk in his eyes by its very accessibility; it will have become just another film and he just another paying customer, now the potential prey to disappointment and anticlimax. To release a film is, in a certain sense, to diminish it

In the United States, as everyone must now be aware, *Batman* is already one of the most commercially successful features ever made, boasting, for its first weekend alone, 'domestic rentals', as they are known in the trade, of an unheard-of forty million dollars, a figure which has had the droll side-effect of making *Ghostbusters*

II, which earned 'only' thirty million over a similar period, look like a flop. It is, in this summer of 1989, the film *one has to have seen*, with the result that, aside from the infants and adolescents and comic-strip devotees who would no doubt have been determined to see it whether it was a success or not, its audience has been significantly (and, for its producers, gratifyingly) inflated by spectators for whom these forty million dollars represent a *production value*, no less than its stars, its sets and its special effects.

The intriguing thing about this kind of mass conditioning as far as Britain is concerned is that, in the recent past, what *one had to have seen* tended to be televisual rather than cinematic in origin – *Brideshead Revisited* and *The Jewel in the Crown*, or *Dallas* and *Dynasty*. It was by declaring oneself in thrall to or else estranged from programmes such as these that one would publicly define one's sociocultural identity, it was within the framework of television, not the, as it then seemed, increasingly marginal and even moribund cinema, that one could, in offices or on construction sites, in a Covent Garden creperie or on the Clapham omnibus, plug oneself into the great mains current of popular taste.

Then, probably around the early eighties, two radical changes took place, of which the principal consequence has been a reversal of traditional roles for the rival mediums. On the one hand, the Hollywood studio chiefs, the so-called moguls, who had always been gamblers by nature, ceased utterly to rely upon, as one says of roulette, a *system* (in this instance, precisely, the studio system) and started instead to wager practically everything they possessed on a handful of 'lucky numbers', in the hope not merely of recouping losses they had sustained elsewhere but ultimately of breaking the bank. In short, they quite consciously set about making films *one had to have seen*. On the other hand, British television became, in both its range (and potential range) of channels and the diversity of its programme schedules, unintelligibly fragmented, partitioned – as a youthful producer once expressed it to me, 'Channel 4-ified'. With only a trio of channels available one could reasonably expect everyone – which is to say, everyone one knew – to have been watching the same programmes. With the advent of a fourth (plus video, cable, satellite channels, etc.) the ecology of our television culture was crucially disturbed and that favourite lunch-hour query of 'Did you see . . .?' would be answered more often than not in the negative.

The ultimate outcome of such an expansion is that television and the cinema have *changed places*, have traded sociocultural functions, even aesthetic strategies. Nowadays a film like *Batman* or *Indiana Jones and the Last Crusade* is unselectively *transmitted* around the country, in cinemas as anonymous, indistinguishable and also multi-channelled as television sets; and, all things considered, the TV viewer will find it easier to elude the tinselly tentacles of *Dallas* and *Dynasty* than the filmgoer those of Indy and Rocky, Superman and now the Caped Crusader. Meanwhile, the more relentlessly TV stations assail him with choice (or what passes for choice), the more, apparently, the confirmed viewer remains faithful to 'his' channel, as once to his local Odeon, which he would dutifully patronise, once or twice a week, virtually irrespective of what was playing there, the medium of the cinema itself being very much more important than the message emitted by any individual film. And just as television used to be routinely exploited by its rival as a vehicle for promoting films, so Hollywood's more commonplace products (*Eight Men Out*, *The Kiss*, and so forth) are now accorded a brief initial theatrical release – a release on parole, you might say – solely to gain the prestige and publicity which continue to be attendant on a West End opening before earning a proper, durable income through video rentals.

Were it not, then, for spectacles like *Batman* and its kind – spectacles *one has to have seen* – cinemas, those once magical pleasure palaces, might well be exclusively reduced to *trailering* films for television consumption.

Reflections on the names of pop groups

I recall once hearing a dirty joke, one so dirty, indeed, it will have to be discreetly abridged in the retelling. A pop group, comprising two young men and a woman, was auditioning in the office of an important concert impresario. To begin with, they were hardly more suggestive in their physical mannerisms than most such acts tend to be. But, once they had properly got into their stride, the three singers whipped themselves up into a frenzy of sexual abandon, attaining heights of troilist ingenuity worthy of some erotomaniac Heath Robinson and depths of bestial debauchery that would not have been disowned by Sade (I mean the marquis, not the pop singer). When it was all over, when the group had crumpled into a drained and dishevelled heap on the carpet in front of him, the impressed impresario turned to their manager and enquired what name they went by. Came the complacent response: 'The Debonaires'.

Those were the days – the innocent days when pop groups would obligingly style themselves the Songsmiths or the Melody-Makers or, slightly more inventively, the Beatles (only slightly, though, for if that name has entered the language, to the point where it is the word 'beetle' that now strikes the casual eye as odd and misspelt, it ought to be remembered that the coinage was originally prompted by an elementary pun on 'beat'). Even someone like myself, who could not be less of an aficionado of pop (I willingly endorse Walter Pater's dictum that all art aspires to the condition of music, but would add *except pop music*), used to be instantly alerted to the nature and style of such groups by their very names, as also by the disconnected little musical staves that jauntily hovered above those names and resembled nothing so much as stray sections of track from an electric train set.

And these days? Near where I live there stands a quasi-permanent construction site whose external barriers have been overspread with flyers advertising what are presumably the latest rock singles and albums. Some of these are by such arcanely named albeit still, to me, vaguely familiar groups as Spandau Ballet, the Cocteau Twins, Eurythmics, and the like. But The Wonder Stuff, for example? Who on earth are they? Or, on an adjacent poster, the free-floating words 'Sugar Cubes' and 'Regina'? Is this poster publicising an album entitled *Sugar Cubes* by a group (or a soloist) named Regina? Or vice versa? And what about, again on one and the same poster, this seemingly random collection of phrases: 'bad dreams' (in lower-case letters) followed by 'senseless timing' and, tucked away in the lower right-hand corner, 'Bomb Disneyland', of all unlikely injunctions? Which is the group and which the name of the album? Who knows? And these: 'SLIDE on tour with Texas', 'W. F. L. the Paul Oakenfold mix', 'tin machine + maggies farm (live) + tin machine' (lower-case letters throughout and *sic* for 'maggies'), etc., etc.? What is one supposed to make of all of that?

The irresistible conclusion is that pop groups, uniquely, are at liberty to call themselves *absolutely anything*. (There could even be a group calling itself 'Absolutely Anything'.) For just consider a few of the cinema's most recent releases. Surely *Slaves of New York, The 'burbs* and *sex, lies and videotape* could equally well be names for pop groups? Any why not *Dangerous Liaisons*? Why not *Rain Man*? Or *A Fish Called Wanda?* Why not *Utz* or *London Fields* or *A History of the World in 10½ Chapters?* Why not British Telecom or Federal Express or *The Sunday Times*? For that matter, why not 'Why Not?'? There is absolutely nothing to prevent a group calling itself 'Why Not?' and for all I know such a group already exists.

In *Reflections on 'The Name of the Rose'*, Umberto Eco summarises the crisis of modernism in a way that may also help us construct a model for the formulation of a theory of pop groups' names. 'The avant-garde destroys, defaces the past,' he says: '*Les Demoiselles d'Avignon* is a typical avant-garde act. Then the avant-garde goes further, destroys the figure, cancels it, arrives at the abstract, the informal, the white canvas, the slashed canvas, the charred canvas. In architecture and the visual arts, it will be the curtain wall, the building as stele, pure parallelepiped, minimal art; in literature, the destruction of the flow of discourse, the Burroughs-like collage, silence, the white page; in music, the passage from atonality to noise to absolute silence.'

The process that Eco describes is centripetal, a flight towards the centre, towards the nub, the essence, the very barest minimum, and it must logically culminate in the apparent destruction of even that minimum. Simultaneously, though, there has been set in motion a reverse process, a movement out from the centre, of a centrifugal rather than centripetal force, one that is now also if less conspicuously in crisis. I started with Surrealists and their stated ambition to undermine, in life as in art, the immemorial foundations of all conscious choice, of rationality itself. But, quite rapidly, the 'Surrealist' degenerated into the merely 'surreal', the bizarre, the funky; acquiring its own clichés (blue cauliflowers by moonlight, etc.), it filtered down to such lesser arts as theatrical set design, fashion, photography and advertising; it infiltrated the world of pop music via the LP sleeve; and, with the naming of pop groups, it would now seem to have reached its own point of saturation.

'W. F. L. the Paul Oakenfold mix', whatever else it might mean, can therefore be seen as a populist counterpart to, let's say, one of Malevich's 'White on White' paintings, confronting the 'nothing goes' of minimalism with the 'anything goes' of what might be called maximalism and demonstrating *ad absurdum* that, in art, whenever everything is possible, nothing is significant.

History's photographic memory

In a London bookshop two or three months ago I bought, as an unbirthday gift to myself, a sumptuously published album of photographs by Robert Mapplethorpe. Although the copy I picked off the display table was cellophane-sealed, I was fully aware of its contents and thus a trifle put out when the sales assistant, on the point of wrapping it up, felt compelled to offer me, in a tone of strangulated diffidence, this unexpected and quite unnecessary forewarning: 'Um . . . you do realise that these are only his portraits?' There was plainly a latent message being imparted which, maybe paranoically, I interpreted as: Please don't come asking for your money back once you discover that the book contains no images of hunky, tattooed male nudes with their genitalia wreathed in chains.

Photography remains a curious, hybrid, paradoxical form (Cecil Beaton once said that photography was not in itself an art but that a photographer could certainly be an artist), a form difficult to practise precisely because it impresses the layman as almost fraudulently easy. For its cluster of authentic creators – as distinct from its legion of amateurs, most of whom, if favoured by circumstance, are perfectly capable of taking a fortuitously good photograph from time to time – the difficulty resides in striving to transcend that inherent facility (what is easiest to do badly is hardest to do well) and attain such a force and intensity of expression that the camera becomes the agent not merely of a perception but of a vision. Even if this is successfully achieved, however, as my little prefatory anecdote bears out, the photographer still risks having his sensibility trammelled by what might be called 'the tyranny of the subject'. It would be wholly unthinkable for the purchaser of an album of Rubens's portraits to be similarly advised on its dearth of fleshy nudes. By contrast, and no matter how dewily (David Hamilton) or abstractly (Bill Brandt) or hallucinatorily (Mapplethorpe) sensitised by the cameraman's eye, photographed nudity is fated to retain much of the unnervingly rude starkness of nudity seen, so to speak, in the flesh.

By its very essence, then, the photographer's relationship to the objective world will always be far less mediated, far less transparent in representational terms, than that enjoyed by virtually any other type of artist. Or, to simplify, it is at least for the general public a question of the pecking order of *by* and *about*: *London Fields* is a novel *by* Martin Amis *about* the London of the nineteen-nineties; whereas a snapshot of the Queen Mother is first and foremost *about* the Queen Mother and only secondarily *by* Cecil Beaton.

This, its hard, incorruptible core of 'documentariness', is photography's weakness but equally the source of its peculiar strength, and the same applies to the related medium of newsreel film. Consider the current spate of television documentaries commemorating the fiftieth anniversary of the Second World War (a spate that, like the conflict itself once it got under way, is unlikely to be all over by Christmas, what with Dunkirk, the Blitz, Pearl Harbor, and so on, patiently queueing up to be memorialised). No fictional reconstruction of the period has ever possessed the oneiric capacity of a newsreel simply and lightly to *touch* the past and give voice to the true silent majority, the dead. No film, no painting, no literary text, has ever so poignantly captured the pathos, the sometimes seriocomic, sometimes haunting, sometimes downright hellish, reality behind the headlines of history: the peaky, pointy-chinned, undernourished faces of evacuee children herded on to station platforms; the breezily gallant secretaries trooping across London's bridges, gas-masks negligently slung over their shoulders as though they had elected *en masse* to tote their skulls about like so many portable intimations of mortality; even, if very much later, those now emblematic mounds of corpses which newsreel footage of the concentration camps has somehow contrived to keep *alive* – alive, that is, in the sense that memories may be said to be alive. If film is, as Cocteau once wrote, the medium by which death is revealed at work, like a colony of bees in a glass hive, it also constitutes a machine for petrifying time, a fountain of eternal youth, and it's the tension generated by these two opposing yet interpenetrating functions that makes all such archive material – history's home movies – so incomparably affecting.

And it isn't impossible that the advent of film has now definitively transformed – and will continue even more radically to transform – our whole attitude towards history, not just the nostalgia-doused history of the recent past but that, more forbidding and rebarbative, of the upper-case H. What, for most of us, do the words 'Battle of Hastings' represent? An ill-digested, only half-heeded history lesson. A textbook illustration in a pseudo-Bayeux style, perhaps. A date, essentially. Please sir, 1066. In 2066, however, even in 3066, those newsreel images of the Belsen and Auschwitz dead will still be resonantly, defiantly, unendurably alive; those thousand-year-old victims of history will have forfeited not an ounce of their humanity or their martyred corporeality; there will be no more mere 'Battles of Hastings'. For it will have become one of the vocations of film – and by then, conceivably, its sole vocation – to render the past *present*.

Umberto E.

There used to exist in this country an amusing and, it would appear, now obsolete fad for self-designated 'laws', which purported to define a few of the more freakish axioms of nature and society. Although, of these, the most notorious by far were Parkinson's Law, the Peter Principle and the ubiquitous and infallible Buggins' Law, my own personal favourite was this forgotten little nugget (perhaps I ought to say McNugget) of truth: 'Everything one eats tastes more or less like chicken.' Surveying the pallid, near-monochromatic spectrum of contemporary British fiction (was it Schopenhauer who said, 'Whenever a new book comes out, I read an old one'?), I am tempted to paraphrase that law and propose the following as currently rather more apt: 'Everything one reads tastes more or less like Anita Brookner.'

These not very singular musings were prompted by a reading of Umberto Eco's new novel, *Foucault's Pendulum*, a quintessential turn-of-the-millennium fiction, a head-spinning extravaganza of mythico-historical speculation, a postmodern folly constructed by a deadly sane man, a devious, wholly unsynopsisable narrative which reads as though it had been modelled on one of those mathematical brain-teasers whose crowning instruction would invariably turn out to be 'now take away the number you first thought of' – a novel, in short, that doesn't taste like chicken.

What concerns me here, though, is not the by now wearisomely rehearsed question of why British writers have long proved incapable of pulling off a *Foucault's Pendulum* (or a *Name of the Rose* or *Bonfire of the Vanities* or *Life A User's Manual*) but the significance in the book's narrative texture – as also, surely, in its very fabrication – of the word processor. So great is that significance, and so great my admiration for Umberto Eco, I might even claim that, if I myself have lately learned how to master (sort of) a word processor, it was partly in order to read Eco 'in the original', as it were, the way English intellectuals used to teach themselves Italian to read Dante in the original.

The word processor in *Foucault's Pendulum* is named Abulafia after an occult philologist, Abraham Abulafia, and is the infernal machine on which the novel's trio of scholarly protagonists recklessly concoct a parallel, archly conspiratorial interpretation of the world's history encompassing the entire two millennia following the birth of Christ. Eco, however, doesn't simply exploit the machine as a plot device, a handy expositional tool. In his third chapter (out of a hundred-and-twenty) – just before the cybernetic Open Sesame is pronounced, before the computer's hitherto uncooperative screen begins 'to fill with words, lines, codes, a flood of communication', and the hero, like the reader, is suddenly granted access to an accumulated store of historico-cabbalistic goodies – we find him ecstatically celebrating its inexhaustible richness of permutations, its wild proliferation of signs and symbols. 'O joy, O new vertigo of difference,' he rhapsodises. 'O my platonic reader-writer racked by a most platonic insomnia, O wake of finnegan, O animal charming and benign.' He compares it to some of the more primitive modes of transporting thought into words: 'If you write with a goose quill you scratch the sweaty pages and keep stopping to dip for ink. Your thoughts go too fast for your aching wrist. If you type, the letters cluster together, and again you must go at the poky pace of the mechanism, not the speed of your synapses. But with him (it? her?) your fingers dream, your mind brushes the keyboard, you are borne on golden pinions, at last you confront the light of critical reason with the happiness of a first encounter.'

Although, once it sets about excavating the most hermetic recesses of history, the circuitous narrative tends slightly to lose sight of Abulafia, it's nevertheless the word processor which remains its playful and at the same time serious central metaphor. And it's by virtue of an almost identical proliferation of signs and symbols that *Foucault's Pendulum* itself functions: its underlying theme – to wit, the fundamental interconnectivity of everything – reflects the very principle that may be said to govern and organise the operation of a computer. Even Eco's occasional stylistic infelicities can be traced back to the ephemerality of a computer text, the faint but indelible impression the user has of words being present on sufferance, swimming back and forth in front of his eyes, flitting almost uncontrollably over his field of vision – the cute way in which, on my own Amstrad, for example, a multisyllabic word will dart across the screen to test whether there is space enough for it to squeeze itself in on the preceding line before changing its mind halfway, exactly as a rounders or baseball player does when he realises he isn't going to make the next base.

Nowadays absolutely everything is channelled through the 'image'; it is no longer the word but the image which has become, or seems destined to become, the basic unit of media communication; and at last, with the advent and dizzyingly expanding popularity of personal computers, words themselves (thoughts, rather) are being transformed into images. (What is, one wonders, the difference between a word and the image of a word?) But the crucial point worth recalling is that every technical innovation brings in its wake a correspondingly innovatory aesthetic. Thus, if Trollope may be said to have written in the 'style' of the goose quill, and Hemingway's short stories and novels were composed in what might be termed a Remingtonian mode, *Foucault's Pendulum*, precisely because Eco has assumed the fullest aesthetic implications of the word processor, that most vertiginous of the writer's props, and no matter how concerned its narrative appears to be with the past, is perhaps the first authentic work of fiction of the twenty-first century.

That siren, silence

In the nineteen-twenties, in characteristically whimsical mood, the French filmmaker René Clair defined the pre-talkie cinema of the period as 'the best means of appreciating silence'. (Clair's enduring attachment to silence was celebrated as late as 1947 in a nostalgic comedy about the early years of the medium, *Le Silence est d'or*.) In a similar vein, I remember, a decade or so ago, a very funny Goodies sketch on television about the shooting of a silent film, which had its cast and crew tiptoeing noiselessly about the set and hissing 'Shhhhh!' at one another. Beyond all the waggishness, however, there is a serious point worth making: that silent films had (almost) as much to do with silence as with film, that silence might even be regarded as having been a genuine asset to the cinema rather than a mere sensual impoverishment, a historical deficiency that could and would be rectified in due time.

Yet, in 1980, at the London Film Festival, the supposed 'deficiency' was indeed redressed, and retroactively. For that year saw the world première of Abel Gance's long-incomplete silent classic *Napoléon* (which, if a film of indisputable importance in and influence on the history of the cinema, is arguably not quite the unconditional masterpiece that it's currently assumed to be) in a version heroically reconstructed by Kevin Brownlow and David Gill in association with Thames Television. And, of course, not content with merely restoring Gance's mutilated epic to something close to its former éclat, Brownlow and Gill made the decision to have it accompanied by a full 'live' orchestra and commissioned Carl Davis both to conduct that orchestra and write a new score for the four-and-a-half-hour marathon performance. Under Waterloo Bridge, coincidentally (for that's where the National Film Theatre is located), Gance's Napoleon finally won his own personal Waterloo against a historical indifference to the fate of hundreds of silent prints mouldering in archives around the world; the enormous critical and public success of this initial venture overrode any lingering doubts on the matter; and, every year since then, some major silent film – *The Thief of Bagdad, The Wind, Broken Blossoms, The General* – has been accorded a similar treatment. This year the film selected is the Harold Lloyd burlesque comedy *Safety Last.*

I dislike being, as a sardonic John Updike once referred to himself in comparable circumstances, the one grouchy fairy invited to the christening, but I simply cannot share the universal enthusiasm. I am ready to acknowledge that in the case of *Napoléon* live musical accompaniment was justified by the gala nature of the event itself and the uncanny synchronism of Davis's Romantic pasticcio with the purplest patches of Gance's (or ExtravaGance's) hagiographical lyricism. (The film might be thought of as its director's *Symphonie Fantastique*.) I acknowledge, too, that the entirely laudable ambition of such screenings is to salvage from the humid archival purgatory of film history a small trove of neglected masterpieces and near-masterpieces, to render them more accessible – more 'user-friendly', as we say nowadays – to a general public. Nevertheless, it does seem to me quite seriously in doubt that the popularity of these Thames Television Classics, as the collection is now called, has engendered any more general appreciation of the silent cinema and its history. A far likelier consequence is that the non-specialist spectator will continue to fight shy of silent films unless they come accompanied by a Carl Davis-conducted orchestra.

The champions of Brownlow and Gill would contend that silent films were never intended to be screened in total silence, that in the twenties, even the teens, of the century some variety of musical accompaniment was always provided. But, aside from the fact that such would have been the producer's, distributor's or exhibitor's intention, not necessarily that of the director, relatively few cinemas of the period, at least outside of major cities, could have afforded to hire more than a solo pianist; and, if there was an ensemble, it would certainly not have been on the scale of what is to be found at the Dominion. The question, however, is not simply one of available means. It's scarcely by chance that film music tends to be qualified by the generic term of 'incidental', a word for which my Roget offers such interesting synonyms as 'circumstantial', 'contingent' and 'inessential'. What cinema pianists supplied was a primitive form of Musak, self-effacing 'furniture music' (the term coined by Satie to categorise the score he composed in 1924 for Clair's avant-garde short *Entr'acte*) that was never meant to be consciously listened to – not, I feel, an accurate description of Davis's full-blown, on occasion overblown, accompaniments.

Even less defensible, in fact a rather ominous development, were recent screenings of Chaplin's *City Lights*, a dialogue-less but not silent film made in 1931, whose original soundtrack was replaced by a live orchestral accompaniment, and Eisenstein's

Alexander Nevsky, a 1938 sound film whose famous Prokofiev score was detached from the soundtrack and conducted *in situ* by Ashkenazy. These experiments were, frankly, a disgrace, the sheerest kitsch, on a level with colorisation.

I am perhaps biased, having had the good fortune to discover the silent cinema at the Cinémathèque Française, whose genial, legendary curator, Henri Langlois, disallowed musical accompaniment of any kind on the grounds that films themselves possessed their own rhythms, their own harmonies, their own music. These screenings at the Palais de Chaillot could be memorably intense, even nerve-racking, experiences; I have never forgotten the films I saw there nearly twenty years ago. For silence carries with it an inherent connotation of respect, as in the funereal ritual of 'a minute's silence'; and it was that sense of respect that enabled those of us in the Cinémathèque's audience to concentrate our minds wonderfully on the film itself and on nothing else. It was also nice for once to have a bit of peace and quiet.

Ologies

It was Nietzsche who in *The Gay Science* wittily conjectured that, just as the nineteenth-century aristocrats he saw around him would hunt for pleasure, where hunting had once been a pursuit of the poor to keep themselves alive, so the new mercantile occupations of the rising bourgeois classes might one day equally become a source, rather, of pure amusement and distraction. He was right: what he prophesied was advertising.

Advertising has never wanted for exegetes, a handful of whom have even been prepared to address the subject in an unabashedly aesthetic and celebratory idiom, but a new publication entitled *You*

Got an Ology? surely constitutes a first: a book actually based on an advertising campaign. What *You Got an Ology?*, co-authored by the actress Maureen Lipman and an advertising copy writer, Richard Phillips, offers the reader in exchange for £8.95 are the twenty scripts of the award-winning British Telecom campaign (including, for the insatiable sort of fanatic, *one that was never filmed*), these scripts being lavishly illustrated, as publishers put it, with colour and black-and-white stills; the family tree of the entire Beattie family ('Beattie', naturally, as in 'BT'); nine pages of 'Mrs Beattie's Recipes and Household Hints' ('Beattie' now, presumably, as in 'Beaton'); two complete storyboards; a five-page spread outlining Lipman's elaborate 'Beattie-fication' (shades, here, of Robert De Niro's heroic transformation into the bloated Jake La Motta of *Raging Bull*); a two-page catalogue of the various prizes picked up by the campaign over the years; and, not least, a preposterously detailed nine-page introduction, 'What Makes Beattie Run', by Phillips.

It is tempting to attribute the existence of such a bizarre confection to sheer *folie de grandeur*, to an advertiser's craving to have his 'creativity' accorded wider recognition, and leave it at that. Inside every fatuous man, to paraphrase Cyril Connolly, there's a slim volume struggling to get out. Yet this 'novelisation' of what, after all, has been no more than a series of crude promotional ploys, amusing enough though they may be to watch, does expose the quite extraordinary power of contemporary TV advertising to generate (or regenerate) myths and fantasies in just the way in which the populist art forms at least have always done.

These days watching what used to be called, with a candour proper to an era less addicted to euphemism than ours, 'commerical' television is not unlike staring fixedly at one of those optical constructions beloved of vulgarising mathematicians in which the black squares of a checkerboard design seem sometimes concave, sometimes convex, depending on how they are registered by the fickle eye. Is it any longer a simple, ungainsayable truth of television that it's the commercials which interrupt the programmes?

That I am not the first to pose the question I know, but might it not be the other way around? And does it ultimately matter?

In fact, commercial breaks bear exactly the same relation to the programmes they punctuate as singles or 38s do to LPs: they are scale models of the larger picture, comparable in every respect save that, simply, of dimension. Thus advertising can boast its domestic sitcoms (precisely the genre of the British Telecom campaign); its diminutive *Dallases* and *Dynasties* (the long-running Gold Blend campaign with a spun-gloss heroine wooed from coffee cup to coffee cup by her male bimbo of a leading man); its nostalgically wispy period reconstructions (the Hovis ads); its chat show personalities (Jerry Hall advertising Bovril); its game shows (those classic interview-test detergent commercials with their irresistible echoes of 'Open the box!' from the old *Take Your Pick* quiz); its classic movies from the golden (or, rather, black-and-white) age of Hollywood (the Holsten skits with Griff Rhys Jones); its documentaries (public-service ads on drug abuse, Aids, Family Credit, and so forth); its Party Political Broadcasts (of which more later); and its musicals, thrillers and indeed anything else that the rival broadcasting channels might have on offer.

But if, paradoxically, advertising has become television's principal rival, it is also advertising rather than television itself (as no doubt was formerly the case) that is now the cinema's true and worst enemy – not only because many of the younger directors, those who comprise what might be called the Campari school of filmmaking, graduated from advertising and still appear more concerned to sell rather than tell a story (e.g. Alan Parker, Hugh Hudson, Tony Scott) but also because, by stealing and debasing the cinema's most time-honoured practices (black-and-white, slow and accelerated motion, etc.) and a few of its more potent myths (Bogart, Monroe) instead of inventing its own, it has dramatically reduced the scope of what is and what is not any longer filmable and rendered us less and less capable of watching a film with an innocent eye.

The real trouble with advertising, however, is that everything it touches, however glancingly, is fated to turn into a product, a commodity whose price-tag is exclusively contingent on fluctuations of supply and demand. Which is what makes the current spate of water commercials in the run-up to privatisation so pernicious. The viewer is invited first of all to regard water as just such a 'product' – a way in which, rightly or wrongly, few of us had ever thought of it before. But because they are also commercials for Thatcherite policies, that viewer is being conditioned at the same time to regard the government as simply another product, a product superior to its rivals by very virtue of the fact that it advertises and they don't, a product to be purchased (or voted for) because it presents itself, like all the best products, 'as seen on TV'. And what is being sold is, of course, an ology.

Eight ways of looking at a coffee-table book

It has become a truism of literary sociology that the material form assumed by a book may influence the way in which the reader consumes it. Reading *Lolita* as a mass-distributed paperback is not quite the same thing as reading it in Maurice Girodias's original Paris edition; and an illuminated manuscript – the book as an irreproducible and hence irreplaceable object – belongs to a cultural mythology very different from, let's say, a *Teach Yourself Sanskrit* guide. Even if, as was the case with *Lolita*, the text itself undergoes only the most infinitesimal variations from one publishing format to the other, it is neither perceived nor read in an identical manner. Similarly, there exist texts that will not be accommodated by just any format: to take an obvious example, who would want to read *The Silence of the Lambs* on *papier Vélin pur fil Lafuma?*

There is, in short, a morphology of books, one that would perhaps merit extended analysis. (It is, as it happens, the current preoccupation of Gérard Genette, the French theorist of language.) But what I would like to consider here is just a single subspecies, one whose increasing visibility on the market, especially in the weeks before Christmas, has not been accompanied by any corresponding intensity of critical scrutiny: that *necessary luxury* of contemporary middle-class consumerism, the coffee-table book.

Since limitations of space preclude the formulation of any precise theory of the coffee-table book, let me offer instead the following eight more or less randomly ordered propositions:

1. To start with, the coffee-table book may be said to imply the pre-existence of a coffee-table as other books (the OED, the Complete Works of Shakespeare, even *The Silence of the Lambs*) carry the implication of a 'library': one need possess neither coffee-table nor library, but the implication persists nevertheless. Its specificity, its public image, is therefore predicated on a social, not to say a class, distinction; it might almost be claimed for it that its existence as a book is preceded by its essence as a status symbol.

2. The social prestige of the coffee-table book is rendered slightly ambiguous, however, by the fact that it tends to be purchased less frequently for oneself than as a gift; more precisely, as a modest two-dimensional correlate of the grander three-dimensional gift that one would like to have made had money been no object. Thus, since the bestowal of a vintage Bentley is out of the question, one presents one's car enthusiast friend with a *book* of vintage Bentleys; given that one cannot possibly afford a trip to the Far East, one treats one's wife to a splendid album of Indonesian temples.

3. As a result, when complacently exhibited on a coffee-table (thereby forever retaining its discrete identity as a gift, as an entity resisting integration into an ensemble of familiar household

effects which, in our unfocused perception of them, will seamlessly dovetail into each other), such a book slyly contrives to serve as a token of a style of gracious living from which its owner has been excluded by petty financial considerations but for which, by dint of innate taste, discernment and breeding, he or she remains eminently fitted.

4. Its presence in a drawing-room (especially when sharing table-top space with what might be called 'coffee-table magazines': *Vogue, Tatler, House and Garden*) also conveys a hint of the doctor's surgery, the embassy antechamber – in a word, the waiting-room. Yet, even if involuntary, this analogy need not be distasteful, for what it suggests, after all, is that owners of coffee-table books belong to that race of superior beings *who keep people waiting*.

5. Inserting a coffee-table book in a bookshelf, vertically, spine outwards, would make no sense at all, as it would be prevented from fulfilling its essential function of self-advertisement. Ostentation is its *raison d'être* and horizontal is its natural state. Indeed, a coffee-table book is so patently *on display* that the role one attributes to it in a drawing-room can be compared without exaggeration to that which it previously had in the bookshop. There it lies, on the coffee-table, waiting to be 'bought' – bought, that is, in the sense of admired, approved and above all, as an external sign, a visible trace, of its owner's culture and affluence, *believed*.

6. The relation that a coffee-table book bears to a 'proper' book is exactly that of a colour supplement to a Sunday newspaper. Although there is in theory nothing to prevent any kind of material from being published in the format of a coffee-table book, and although a colour supplement may often devote a photo-spread to one of those major, even tragic, news items which are likely to be more fully documented within the body of the newspaper (famine in Africa, guerilla wars in Latin America), the inescapable *textural* glossiness of both types of publication seems to mirror a corresponding *textual* superficiality. What in fact discourages the reader from engaging at any real emotional level with the book's subject-matter, however 'shocking', what indelibly colours

his perception of it, is colour itself. Coffee-table books are as a rule in colour; and, as Barthes said, 'colouring the world is always a means of denying it'.

7. One does not borrow a coffee-table book, just as it would be presumptuously unreasonable to expect to borrow a jade Buddha or a costly executive toy. Nor is it likely to be critically reviewed (except, in bulk, at Christmas), or republished as a paperback, consulted by students, listed in bibliographies, lovingly learnt by heart, quoted from or reread. A single reading, if that, is ordinarily enough to exhaust the practical or connoisseurial advantages to be gained from it by its eventual owner. And from its publisher's point of view it holds out a grand total of two marketing options: it can be sold and it can be remaindered.

8. The coffee-table book is, in the last analysis, the modern equivalent of those hollow Morocco-bound tomes which handily *papered* the walls of nineteenth-century libraries (as an impresario is said to 'paper' a half-empty theatre): it is an accessory, a mere prop, its basic theatricality more or less exempting it from containing anything at all.

The Poet Laureate of childhood

I recall, as an infant, firmly believing that the conductor Leopold Stokowski, who makes a brief personal appearance in the opening sequence of *Fantasia*, was himself a cartoon character and that the name 'Walt Disney' was just one of the several aliases assumed by Father Christmas. For me, therefore – as also, I imagine, for many of my contemporaries – seeing one of Disney's full-length cartoons again, as I occasionally do, is rather like being confronted with the Ghost of Christmas Past. Amazingly, though, in spite of the rival charms of E. T. and Superman, Indy and Batman, the old enchanter's prestige would seem to have been dented less than one had imagined: the very latest of the studio's cartoons, *The Little Mermaid*, has just opened in America to an unexpectedly triumphant critical and commercial reception.

Why so? Beyond its frequent visual and technical sophistication, its virtuoso effects of guttering candles, gliding shadows and huge, translucent tears, three (related) factors seem to me crucial to an understanding of the enduring bewitchment of Disney's work, and they might be encapsulated as follows:

One, there is a charming comic strip by the French satirist Sempé, of a little girl and boy lolling on a sofa in front of a wanly flickering TV screen and being hypnotised into a state of semi-conscious lethargy by the medium's audiovisual stream-of-consciousness (or unconsciousness). Nothing, it appears, can animate the four glazed little pinpricks of their eyes, not newsreel footage of atrocities in the Middle East nor the gung-ho sadism of some Second World War movie nor the more fastidious violence of a typical French *policier*. Then, suddenly, Disney's Snow White, as rudimentary a human figure as might be found in one of Sempé's own drawings, is being pursued through the forest by the wicked Queen, and the two diminutive and now saucer-eyed viewers are shrieking their heads off and cowering behind the sofa in terror.

Two, the last time I myself saw *Snow White and the Seven Dwarfs* was in Paris a few years ago, in a dubbed version. Although I was slightly put out by the dwarfs' hitherto unsuspected command of French, dubbing did strike me for once as a legitimate device, given that the children who made up two-thirds of the audience would have been foxed by subtitles. But what brought me up short – what, I have to say, actually shocked me – was the fact that in the dwarfs' bedroom the names carved on the ends of their wooden beds were not Dopey, Grumpy, and so forth, but their French equivalents, Simplet, Grincheux and the like. (The Disney company had presumably prepared separate versions for some of the major foreign-language markets.)

Three, nearly thirty years ago, when his facial features were very much less familiar in this country than they since became, Walt Disney himself was a guest on the 'celebrity spot' of the panel show *What's My Line?* On his entering the studio the public barely reacted; once he had 'signed in', however, and there are few signatures more famous than his, there arose a tremendous burst of applause.

Now, the truth demonstrated by Sempé's gag is that children, no matter how jaded they might have become by exposure to the adult world's capacity for inflicting pain, have never ceased to respond to certain more naïve and primary archetypes of aggression. And since these archetypes were necessarily man-made, there seems no good reason why some gifted twentieth-century fantasist, an heir to Grimm, Perrault and Andersen, should not have gone on making them. The fact nevertheless remains that, in literature, Barrie was probably the very last creator to have devised, in Peter Pan, a myth of near-universal resonance – in the sense that later collections of fairy-tales have tended to be regarded as pastiches of a genre to which his work belongs unambiguously. It has in consequence been left to Disney to retrieve and reinvent the genre for our own century, and so definitively has he done so that it's now all but impossible for us to visualise Snow White or Pinocchio or Cinderella other than in the animated imagery in which he fashioned them.

Which is why I was so startled by the weird, foreign names on the dwarfs' beds, as startled as a child would be if, on the umpteenth retelling of the tale, he or she were brusquely informed that the dwarfs numbered not seven but six. Being far less susceptible than live-action films to the evolution of fashions in visual texture, vocal delivery and physical appearance, cartoons possess an almost ageless immutability; hence the sleek, schematic seamlessness of Disney's puff-pastry world has become the ideal vehicle for fairy-tale intemporality.

And there, perhaps, is the crux of the matter. Although we may know otherwise, we find it difficult even as adults not to endorse the common misconception of fairy-tales as essentially authorless artefacts. *Snow White*, for example. Was it part of a collection by Perrault or the brothers Grimm? The answer is Grimm, but the distinction is of little importance. Few of us have read it in its original version anyway; and, for those who have, that reading remains an experience oddly detachable from the more autonomous and free-floating form in which it has most profoundly affected them.

As far as most of us are concerned, Disney's films, too, are authorless artefacts, not really 'directed'. Walt's own features may be more widely recognisable nowadays than they were to the public of *What's My Line?* back in the fifties, we still don't really know what to make of him as an artist. He seemed to do no more than hover vigilantly above the fabrication of the work that bore his signature – as Perrault and the brothers Grimm above the folk-tales that inspired them – less as a creator, an *auteur*, than as a benign, avuncular and spectral overseer. So that, if the best of that work – notably, that quartet of early masterpieces, *Snow White*, *Pinocchio*, *Dumbo* and *Bambi* – is as fresh and sparkling now as it must have appeared to its first dazzled spectators all of fifty years ago, it's no doubt because it has become as much ours as his own.

Noises off

Cocteau, in *Mon Premier Voyage*, an enchanting travel memoir dating from 1936 (when he was commissioned by a Parisian newspaper, several years before S. J. Perelman, Nicholas Coleridge and Michael Palin, to retrace the footsteps of Phileas Fogg and circumnavigate the globe in eighty days), recounts the following magnificent fable, which might fairly be described as the 1002nd tale of the Arabian Nights.

A princess and a poor sandalmaker fall in love and, although dutifully putting up the show of parental resistance traditional to every such liaison, the princess's father, the Sultan, eventually consents to bless their union. A splendid wedding banquet is held, to which the potentates of Persia, India and far Cathay are all naturally invited. Alas, at the very height of the festivities, with his demure and virginal bride seated beside him, the poor sandalmaker involuntarily and all too audibly breaks wind. Ashen-faced, he brusquely rises from the table and rushes out of the palace; then, gathering up his paltry belongings, departs the city altogether. He traverses mountains, valleys, rivers and plains and, after journeying many, many days and nights, arrives at a tiny village located far from the capital. In this village he marries, has lots of children and settles down to ply his humble trade.

Years later, an old man now, the sandalmaker expresses a wish to see once more, just once before he dies, the city in which he passed his youth. So he traverses plains, rivers, valleys and mountains and, after journeying many, many nights and days, arrives at the capital. But what he discovers is a city in ruins, its walls crumbling, its avenues weed-infested, its monuments crawling with chimpanzees. And when he approaches a solitary old beggar woman and asks her when all of this happened, she replies, with a weary expression suggesting that it was ever thus, 'The year of the fart.'

If I have related the story at such length, it is, in the first place, because I consider it to be entirely worthy of its 1001 predecessors; in the second, because farting is currently fashionable, if that's the word, with the English National Opera's pioneering 'scratch 'n' sniff' production of Prokofiev's *The Love for Three Oranges* at the Coliseum; in the third, because it represents an almost (but, as I shall demonstrate, not quite) unique instance in which breaking wind is deployed in an art form to other than low comic effect.

Rather than all the usual candidates – namely, incest, death and money – farting is surely our last surviving social, cultural and aesthetic taboo. Most of us are now cavalierly prepared to admit to masturbation (if not precisely to 'masturbating', then at least to 'having masturbated', oh once or twice, a long, long time ago, during those dim, grim years of adolescence when one practically required a ration card to have any sex at all); by contrast, rare would be the individual at ease regaling a dinner-table with a racy anecdote about letting rip at some amusingly inopportune moment. Even in the very few films in which a character is actually heard to fart (whether in one of the episodes of the *Carry On* cycle or, appropriately enough, in Pasolini's 1974 version of the *Arabian Nights*), the noise on the soundtrack is clearly, deliberately, intended to resonate in an inauthentic and tin-trumpety manner, as though the performer to whom the fart is attributed were unwilling to have it produced by a human surrogate, for fear some innocent spectator be incapable of making the distinction between him and his stand-in.

The fact is that we chilly, puritanical Northern souls tend to treat the waist as the Equator of the body; and although we have for the most part succeeded in taming and colonising those unruly tropical regions situated below the belt, every so often the natives become restless and, before open revolt is permitted to break out, we find ourselves obliged to dispatch a unit of crack troops up the Khyber Pass. But there again, as you see, even when one tries to write on the subject in serious terms, it is all but impossible to avoid a note of vulgar comic innuendo.

Yet it certainly can be done, as Jean Genet proved in the quite unforgettable scene of his novel *Funeral Rites* in which, if memory serves, a middle-aged woman-of-the-world locks her bedroom door, stretches out on her bed and ecstatically liberates her intestinal gases. Suddenly her (very much younger) lover taps from without. He cannot understand why the door has been locked; she, for her part, is petrified at the notion of his entering the room before the air has cleared. Actually, I've forgotten what happens next, but the horrifying pathos of the heroine's plight has already frozen the reader to the core of his being.

Until farting has been properly demystified, then, it will continue to be, outside of broad farce, no laughing matter. For consider the coda to Cocteau's little parable: as the poor sandalmaker is about to take his leave of the ancient crone of a beggar woman, it suddenly dawns on him that she is none other than the princess to whom he had been betrothed.

Closed circuits

Do you remember a once favourite device of *Radio Times* covers? A silver-haired, twinkle-eyed old buffer, a kind of plain-clothes Santa Claus, snug in an armchair in front of a glowing open fire with an apple-cheeked, pyjama-clad grandchild on his lap, would be holding up a copy of the *Radio Times* on whose cover could be seen a reduced version of the same silver-haired, twinkle-eyed old buffer holding up a copy of the *Radio Times* on whose cover could be seen an even tinier silver-haired, twinkle-eyed old buffer holding up a copy of the *Radio Times* on whose now barely distinct cover . . . and so, were space to permit, *ad infinitum*.

This Russian-doll nesting structure (long since abandoned, alas, like so much else that used to constitute its quaintness and charm, by the journal in question) may be designated in several different ways – infinite recursion, circularity, self-referentiality, *mise en abyme* – and is, in less trivial guise, one of the fundamental practices of high postmodernism. But if it has disappeared from the layouts of TV listings magazines, it continues, curiously, to influence television itself. There was, for example, an amusing scene in the Comic Strip's recent *GLC* parody, in which, besieged in County

Hall, Ken Livingstone (played by Robbie Coltrane playing Charles Bronson) finds out who his true friends are during a climactic shootout with the armies of the Thatcherite night. Eric Heffer, Arthur Scargill and Tony Benn manfully respond to the call; Neil Kinnock welshes out, so to speak; and the beleaguered Livingstone finally turns to a teeshirted group cowering in a corner: 'And you, you alternative comedians – are you with us?' There they all are, Dawn French and Jennifer Saunders, Nigel Planer and Adrian Edmondson, playing themselves within the context of a show in which they also play a cluster of (very lightly) fictionalised politicians. (Needless to say, they collectively mumble something about a pressing lunch date with Michael Grade at the Groucho and manage to squirm out of the impending confrontation).

An even more striking instance of narrative circularity was demonstrated by one of the latest episodes of *The Gary Shandling Show*, an American import seldom remarked upon by television critics, badly promoted by the BBC and yet intriguing precisely for the sly, systematic style in which it subverts the immemorial conventions of situation comedy. Briefly, the situation of the episode in question was as follows: The little boy who lives next door to Gary wins a local poetry competition and his prize is a trip to Hollywood and a chance to watch the videotaping of . . . *The Gary Shandling Show* – which is to say, of the selfsame episode of the show in which all these events are taking place. Thus we, the viewers, find ourselves watching the little boy sitting in the audience watching the show of which he himself happens to be one of the main participants; and it's a simple enough matter extending the recursion one stage further by imagining the young actor himself sitting at home watching the show in which he himself is part of the studio audience simultaneously watching the show.

These examples are diverting enough in themselves, but they also underscore the increasingly self-referential essence of the medium to which they belong – or, rather, the medium as it currently exists in this country, prior to the convulsive upheaval of deregularisation. Noël Coward once said that television was for appearing on, not for watching, yet the distinction is becoming an ever finer one. Indeed, I have sometimes wondered – in the absence of (to my knowledge) any statistics on the matter – exactly what percentage of the population has actually *appeared on television.* I am not referring to the medium's professionals, those who work in television in one capacity or another and who themselves must number in their tens of thousands. I mean those who have swum more ephemerally (if, in their own minds, no doubt indelibly) into a TV cameraman's ken: contestants on quiz shows; audiences for *Question Time*; striped-shirt-sleeved City brokers; striking ambulance workers; high-street shoppers worried about mortgage rates and poll tax bills; high-street retailers worried about the continuing absence of high-street shoppers; Southern Region commuters outraged at the latest above-the-inflation-rate hike in the price of a season ticket; by-electors; orderly lines of tots waving diminutive Union Jacks at Diana and Fergie; next-door neighbours interviewed on their doorsteps and informing news reporters that 'He was a nice enough fellow – a very quiet type, though, kept pretty much to himself . . .' – in short, all the myriad manifestations of the man and woman in the street.

The point is that, by now, *everyone* in this country must either have at one time or another been on television or else know someone who has. And if McLuhan was right about the 'global village' that the media have created, perhaps too much emphasis has been placed on television's global pretensions and too little on its villagey intimacy.

At its worst, such cosy circularity will engender a debilitating species of sociological inbreeding. Like a caged budgerigar blissfully prattling away to its own reflection, the viewer may on occasion be caught staring into the looking-glass of his own prejudices. At its best, however, British television has proved to be an unsurpassed medium for democratising our sense of national identity and even national unity. *It speaks to us of ourselves.* And when it truly does become global, when we are at last able to switch from language to language, and from culture to culture, the way we can do at present with radio (but who does?), what will have been lost for ever is a unique, because nationwide, form of closed-circuit television.

Call no man happy

'A well-known scientist (some say it was Bertrand Russell) once gave a public lecture on astronomy.'

That is the first sentence of Stephen Hawking's *A Brief History of Time*. I quote it here not because I regard it as of especial interest or elegance but because it confirms an axiom I once formulated, an axiom which proposed that no matter how arduous a book turned out to be in the reading – and Hawking's book, even if promoted as a vulgarisation, raises questions already so ethereally arcane for most readers as to be wellnigh unvulgarisable – its very first sentence would always be child's play. (Compare the first sentence of Heidegger's *What is Philosophy?* – 'With this question we are touching on a theme which is very broad, that is, widespread' – with its thirty-fifth – 'For whoever wishes to designate philosophy as irrational thereby takes the rational as a measure of limitation and, what is more, does it in such a way as again to take for granted what reason is'.)

A Brief History of Time happens to be the book I am reading at the moment. Since it was originally published two years ago, there is, to be sure, nothing very topical about it. But I would justify focusing on it in this article by virtue of the fact that, remarkably, it has not yet quit the bestseller lists; that time, by definition, can hardly avoid being topical; that, finally, there is topicality and topicality: within the time-frame addressed by Hawking, after all, those two years represent something like a microfraction of a nanosecond, whatever that is, in the history of the universe. What intrigues me most about the book, though, is the amazing frequency with which it prevails upon the lay reader (this lay reader at least) to raise his eyes dreamily from the complicated page, the amazing regularity with which it prompts him to indulge his own, usually quite unscientific reveries on the matter of time.

These reveries may be completely peripheral to Hawking's *propos*, as was the case with the little maxim cited above; or the fact that, bemired in one of the book's more fiendishly abtruse passages, I started to imagine, Monty Pythonishly, the possibility of some foolhardy contestant on *Mastermind* choosing Hawking's theory of the unification of physics, the so-called 'theory of everything', as his specialised subject and taking the programme's full half-hour running time simply to answer the first question.

But they are perhaps a trifle more fruitful when (if, from a physicist's point of view, in a frivolously illegitimate manner) they seek to relate an abstract concept like Einsteinian relativity to humanity's own direct and daily experiencing of time. Most of us, in fact, have always been obscurely conscious that linear chronology is nothing more or less than the alphabetical order of time, a convention almost as pure and arbitrary as that which has been imposed on language. That common lament of forty-year-olds – how much more terrifyingly swiftly time passes than when one was younger – can thus be elucidated by the following equation. For a child of ten a single calendar year represents exactly one-tenth of his life as it has been lived up to that point. For an adult of forty, on the other hand, that same year represents merely one-fortieth. In accordance, therefore, with Adair's Second Axiom, it will pass exactly four times more quickly for the adult than for the child. Indeed, it has been my general finding that, the longer I live, the more alert I become to an *inflation* of time, as of money: which is to say, I seem these days to be able to do as little in an hour as I am able to buy with a pound; and, once one or the other (the hour or the pound) has been 'broken into', I find I have practically no change left. Time is, as they say, money, except that no one will ever be a millionaire of time.

One's reveries, finally, may be cultural in origin. And, in that category, I would like to offer gratis, to some playwright in quest of a plot, an idea which once occurred to me for a drama in the tradition of J. B. Priestley's 'time plays' – plays that, it has to be said, have themselves not well stood the test of that time of which they made such a production number. With this putative play, moreover, comes its appropriately Priestleyan title, *Call No Man Happy* (from Sophocles's 'Call no man happy until the last page of his life has been turned').

So: The curtain rises on what is patently a sickroom (a huge bed stage-centre, a nurse dozing in an armchair with a Mills and Boon in her lap, heavy drawn curtains, filtered 'dark' light) and the drama centres upon the very last five minutes in the life of its protagonist. (Since the play itself would run the traditional sort of length, there might also be, visible onstage, a clock whose hands would take a couple of hours to complete just five minutes of theatrical time – a typically Priestleyan *trouvaille*, if I say so myself.) It's a happy man who is dying, dying at midnight on the eve of his seventieth birthday, his prescribed threescore-and-ten, dying in the blissfully secure knowledge that he is loved by his wife, worshipped by his children, admired and respected by his colleagues. Yet, just five minutes before he breathes his last, *and only then*, he discovers that his wife has been unfaithful to him with virtually all of his close friends, that his children despise him for having forced them to enter the family business when their personal ambitions lay elsewhere and that his colleagues have perpetually had to fend off bankruptcy proceedings as a result of his own professional incompetence.

And this would be the question posed by the play: Has such a man enjoyed sixty-nine years, eleven months, twenty-nine days, eleven hours and fifty-five minutes of happiness, followed by a mere five minutes of unhappiness – in which case he is truly to be envied? Or, in the light of these literally eleventh-hour revelations, has his *whole* existence been an unhappy one? Think before you answer. Take your time.

O'Hanlon in Amazonia

The exiled Latin-American filmmaker Raul Ruiz once assured me that his earliest recollection, dating from his infancy in a hamlet in up-country Chile, was actually of being 'discovered' and even 'claimed' by a party of English explorers while he was playing with a spinning-top on the veranda of his parents' small ranch home – explorers whom he conjured up for me as scanning the horizon in Jungle Jim safari suits, earnest lily-white palms cupped over shining brows.

Well, maybe so. But whether or not the anecdote is genuine – or, rather, whether or not the incident occurred in quite so ludicrously stereotypical a fashion – the fact remains that, because of *something* that happened in his childhood, Ruiz retains to this day a bemused abhorrence of the English for what he regards as their complacently imperialist assumption that, whereas European nations have been dignified with a proper history, those of South America (and the Third World in general) can claim little more than a geography. He abhors them, above all, for their insatiable and incorrigible colonising tendencies, even in an era (if it took place at all, the incident in question would have taken place in the early fifties) when the main effect of these tendencies was to reduce a once vigorous, albeit inevitably imperialist and often avowedly mercenary, tradition of expeditionary adventurism to its grotesque parody.

If, in their own way, the characteristic botherations of airborne tourism such as we have come to know them in the late twentieth century – the crowded sky, the elbow-grinding, ankle-cramping crucifixion of charter flights, the ricey-dicey blandness of airline meals, that moment halfway across the Atlantic, say, when one's long-suffering legs start to feel like a matching pair of Möbius strips – may strike the weary (and, in the most literal sense, world-weary) traveller as scarcely less punishing than those of late nineteenth-century pedestrian globe-trotting, they are, nevertheless, botherations contingent upon an ideal of gregarity rather than of isolation. Instead of going where no one has ever gone before, we generally find ourselves going where everyone else is going as well. And one consequence of such swarming self-congregation is that, among the English, there would appear to be an immense residue of nostalgia for those aching immensities of time and space, those glinting harmonies of sun, sea and sand, that one associates with Freya Stark, Robert Byron, Wilfred Thesiger *et al*, whose classic works of travel writing have been once more made available in a wave of re-issues. Nor can there be much doubt that this strictly geophysical nostalgia is intimately linked with a more profound, more overtly ideological and reactionary nostalgia for a world in which such adventurism was still possible, even laudable, a world in which 'the wogs begin at Calais', a world appropriated as the oyster of the English, destined as they were by innate superiority of breeding, intelligence and pigmentation to tread the unbeaten path, just as other races were there mostly to be trodden upon.

Yet a little volume recently come my way demonstrates that the ever-increasing importance of ethnography in the contemporary history of ideas has not entirely cramped the style of the old-fashioned English explorer. This is Redmond O'Hanlon's *In Trouble Again*, an indefatigably jocular account of his expedition into Amazonia in search of the Yanomami, the largest uncorrupted tribe of Indians still to be found in the rain forest and also apparently 'the most violent people on earth'. O'Hanlon, who is shown on the book's jokey jacket peering owlishly from out of some cartoonish undergrowth, is evidently a bit of a card, his role in the narrative less that of its mere author than of some eccentric television personality *à la* David Bellamy, but he has at least had the honesty to inscribe the Jungle Jim self-parody referred to above into the very textures of his account. And the paperback edition comes graced with encomiums from satisfied, indeed ecstatic, customers: Martin Amis is quoted, in an unmistakably Amisian effusion, as finding it a 'hallucinogenic, scrotum-tightening' read.

No one seems to have wondered, however, whether there might not be something faintly offensive today about the whole concept of an 'explorer', about the whole concept of an Englishman describing, in unrepentantly comic and Eurocentric terms, as though it comprised an exotic collection of I. T.s (or infra-terrestrials), the sort of closed and isolated community from which, as we know from the great modern anthropologists, there can be so much to learn about the ritual-based structures of our own society. No one seems to find it untoward that O'Hanlon should be more interested in breezily detailing his seriocomic misadventures *en route* than in enlightening the reader on what he finds when he gets there. As Amis again is quoted as saying (although presumably as a compliment), 'When Redmond O'Hanlon undertakes his gruelling quests, he isn't really seeking the White Rhino of Borneo or the Amazonian Yanomami. He is seeking the Great Travel Book.' Precisely.

The sterile critic

The very first critical article I was ever commissioned to write – for a university magazine in the mid-sixties – was a review of Alain Resnais's film *L'Année dernière à Marienbad.* The article was never published. In fact, it never even got written.

There I was, seated in the front row of the stalls, mesmerised by the hieratic CinemaScope images, as of a chess game shot by a fashion photographer, of an exquisite, ethereally filmy Delphine Seyrig swanning through the marmoreal salons and corridors of the spa in which that most enigmatic of movies is set – when, suddenly, from the balcony above me, there resounded an anguished, outraged shriek, couched in a Glaswegian idiom so thick as wholly to defy onomatopoeic mimicry: 'Sorry? *Sorry?* The man pukes all over my wife's brand new fur coat and all *he* says is Sorry!' It mortifies me to confess that I fled from the auditorium and informed my editor in a still trembling voice that I would need at least a week to recover before I could once more face the film. Naturally, I was thrown out on my overly sensitive ear, and my career as a critic was set back by practically a decade.

Since then I feel I have become a rather more robust example of the breed, and am thus a tiny bit offended by a television commercial, recently screened throughout the metropolitan area, for the London *Evening Standard*. The scene of this commercial is an archetypal suburban semi-detached and its two principal characters are a no less archetypally middle-aged, middle-class and middlebrow husband and wife. When we first see them, the husband's nose is buried in the newspaper in question, while his wife is claiming rather tetchily not to know what he finds to read in it. At which point their doorbell rings and through the increasingly cramped confines of their living-room charge the human (if heavily caricatured) embodiments of the newspaper's various sections, with sportsmen representing the sports columns, a posturing model representing the fashion page, a peruked Pepysian diarist representing the gossip column and, bringing up the rear, with plummy shrieks of 'Don't forget the critics!', a pair of epicene creatures, both of them, as they say, *d'un certain âge*, both of them, too, sporting that now slightly passé signifier of preening gayness: a silk neck scarf.

Like most such playlets, which have generally less than a minute to promote their product, the *Evening Standard* commercial is dependent upon a set of handy cultural connotations as short-cuts to comprehension; which must mean that someone, somewhere, judged that what would most rapidly connote a critic in the eyes of the average viewer was the campy flamboyance that it seems most people continue to equate with homosexuality. Yet, although I have no statistics at my disposal, and my own experience is necessarily confined to my own areas of competence, I very much doubt whether the incidence of flamboyant homosexuality among the critical fraternity runs conspicuously high, and can only surmise that a parallel is being drawn between two types of *sterility*.

What the ad would appear to be saying, in short, is that the critic, like the homosexual, is creatively or procreatively impotent. Himself deprived of issue, he takes a crabbed sort of comfort in criticising (or, rather, which for many a right-thinking person amounts to the same thing, bitching about) the offspring of others, whether these be cultural or human. Or else, in a more benign manifestation of the species, he has recourse to an attribute that has traditionally been regarded as a feminine preserve: the blazoning of artistic taste. The critic is therefore (by that false 'therefore' of reactionary orthodoxy) the pathetic parody of an artist, just as the homosexual is widely held to be the parody either of a woman (the silk neck scarf) or of a *real* man (the crew-cut and trim moustache of the so-called 'clone' look).

That would be calumny enough, but even more disheartening is the fact that the critic has had of late to square off with an entirely new adversary: the columnist. Downmarket and up, in both the tabloids and the qualities, there has been an amazing proliferation of columnists in recent years, and it can scarcely be by chance that their prominence has increased in proportion as that of critics has declined. And if the reductive signifier of the critic is the silk neck scarf, the columnist's (here again, I suspect, with scant statistical support) is that emblematic prop of bluff, Priestleyan masculinity, the pipe.

No nancy boy, you can be sure, is the columnist, but a prosy and argumentative chappie paid good money to talk good sense – which, in practically all of the tabloids and not a few of the qualities, means simply reinforcing the reader in his or her own already ossified prejudices. Whereas it's a form of professional deformation in the critic endlessly, on occasion almost neurotically, to temper his opinions with such conventional qualifiers as 'in a sense' and 'to a certain degree' and 'it might be argued that', the typical columnist has no truck with such effete equivocations. 'Come off it!' he snorts at whatever might be the object of his codified contempt; or else 'Isn't that just typical!' he agrees with the reader before the latter has even had time to formulate an autonomous opinion. And if the whole sexual analogy seems a somewhat farfetched one, consider merely the 'doyen' of newspaper columnists, the grotesque John Junor, and the importance that both critics and homosexuals have tended to assume in the demonology of his columns.

The first fifteen minutes of Shakespeare

I wonder if anyone else feels, as I do, when meeting 'new people' at a dinner or cocktail party, that the conventional chronology of these awkward encounters might with pleasure and profit be reversed. As things currently stand, one is presented, via a brief exchange of names, to one's putative interlocutor, who is probably at that moment endeavouring to manoeuvre a petit-four off his paper plate and into his mouth without upturning his glass of white wine; one swaps, in as yet a suitably tentative fashion, a few inoffensive generalities or else, if one happens to belong to the same professional milieu, the usual tribal pleasantries and unpleasantries; and, with luck, after fifteen minutes or so, one has eventually started to take the measure of one's latest acquaintance. By which stage of the conversation, one has already, humiliatingly, forgotten his mumbled and only half-heeded name.

I have often thought that a much more sensible solution (akin to what is termed in the cinema a pre-credit sequence) might be for one to chat blithely away to one's fellow partygoer for that ice-breaking quarter of an hour and then, and only then, only when one is beginning to comprehend something of the person with whom one is dealing, when his or her identity has at last acquired the necessary modicum of social and cultural context, would one proceed with the exchange of names.

I was reminded of that situation the other day at the Barbican while watching the new Royal Shakespeare Company production of *All's Well That Ends Well* and experiencing a (to me) now all too familiar malaise – the malaise of what I call 'the first fifteen minutes of Shakespeare'. It's a sensation I am chary of publicly airing, as I have yet to hear anyone else, be it a layman or a professional critic, confess to sharing it. (But it's one of the minor hazards facing columnists that they are fated to remain tantalisingly uncertain as to where their own experience ends and universal experience begins.)

Let me, notwithstanding, plunge in. The scene, then, is the main theatre of the Barbican, where the curtain is about to rise (metaphorically, as the RSC has dispensed with drop-curtains) on one of Shakespearazade's less frequently told tales, *All's Well That Ends Well*. The title, naturally, rings an almost too immediate bell – but the play itself? Hum. It's a comedy, or so that title would seem to intimate, perhaps one of those dark, saturnine comedies which invariably turn out, in the canon, to be 'late' and whose plots one always tends to forget? No matter, its secrets will soon be divulged, as the lights are dimming and a quartet of unidentified characters have already stepped on to the stage, two of them male, two of them female, shifting to and fro in restlessly choreographed movements. I lean forward in my seat, my ears prick up expectantly, and this is what I hear:

A: *In delivering my son from me, I bury a second husband.*

B: *And I, in going, madam, weep o'er my father's death anew; but I must attend his majesty's command, to whom I am now in ward, evermore in subjection.*

C: *You shall find of the king a husband, madam; you, sir, a father. He that so generally is at all times good, must of necessity hold his virtue to you, whose worthiness would stir it up where it wanted rather than lack it where there is such abundance.*

And so it goes. For quite fifteen minutes (sometimes possibly even longer – it's hard to tell in the dark), while all about me my neighbours seem utterly in thrall to the unfolding drama, like those travellers one meets on a lengthy rail journey who instantly close their eyes and fall asleep whereas one's own eyes are only ever closed for form's sake, I appear to be entirely alone in feeling like raising my hand, rising to my feet in a doubtless startled and hushed auditorium and making a plaintive yet challenging request to the performers: 'Come again?'

I admit it, since no one else will: for the first fifteen to twenty minutes of any of Shakespeare's plays but the weariest old warhorses, the *Hamlets* and *Othellos* and *As You Like Its*, I have absolutely no idea what is going on. Who *are* these people? What *are* they talking about? What on earth does 'He that so generally is at all times good, must of necessity hold his virtue to you, whose worthiness would stir it up where it wanted rather than lack it where there is such abundance' mean? And is it going to be crucial to my understanding of the play? More generally, why does this happen to me only with Shakespeare (never with Jonson or Sheridan or Shaw)? And might there not be some means devised whereby spectators like me could sit on, as in the cinema, and watch the first fifteen minutes over again?

To be sure, the malaise does at last pass, and I am no less prepared to admit to luxuriating in those ineffably euphoric moments, fifteen to twenty minutes in, when I become conscious that the fog has indeed started to dissipate and I no longer feel as terrifyingly dense as I did – moments almost (but not quite, no, truly, not quite) worth the agony that preceded them.

And that is really all I wanted to say. I realise I have left myself no room properly to analyse the phenomenon or else explore audience psychology on a less subjective and anecdotal basis (which might have been pertinent in a week which has seen the opening of a play dealing with just such a theme, Michael Frayn's new farce *Look, Look*). But I don't care. This article has been therapeutic for me. I've got the thing off my chest and I feel better for it. In short, all's well that ends well.

Oscar

Oscar Wilde. The name itself seems indissolubly linked to a notion of celebrity. (It is inconceivable that a chartered accountant or a stationmaster be called Oscar Wilde.) And, curiously, one says 'Oscar' as often as 'Wilde', Oscar Wilde being one of the few artists in any field with whom posterity has remained on first-name terms. (No one, to my knowledge, has ever thought to say 'Matthew' for Matthew Arnold or 'George', heaven forbid, for George Eliot.)

But why should Oscar Wilde have become so apparently indispensable to these British and brutish Isles? Only recently we have been treated to not one but two one-man dramatisations of his life, in which he is personified by, respectively, Donald Sinden and

Stephen Rea (just as, by an odd coincidence, there once happened to be two film biographies of him on concurrent release, one of them starring Peter Finch, the other starring Robert Morley); to Steven Berkoff's luridly monochromatic production of *Salome* at the National Theatre; to Richard Ellmann's new, massive biography; to a separate biography of Oscar's devoted confidant, Robert Ross; and, of course, to regular 'mountings' of his plays at Chichester, the Haymarket and other such posh venues. (Oscar's work, unlike Beckett's or Brecht's or even Shakespeare's, is invariably said to be 'mounted'.)

But, again, why? For Oscar's achievement, if emancipated from the often trumpery efflorescence of his life, was a distinctly patchy one. It's true, he wrote the greatest comedy of manners in the language (and probably any other language). He wrote *The Picture of Dorian Gray*, which, with all its absurdities, its stylistic excrescences, its veinily purplish patches, is still the most enthralling second-rate novel in English literature. He wrote a cluster of brilliant essays. And he wrote, as his sole posthumous (which is to say, post-prison) work, *The Ballad of Reading Gaol*, a moving and quotable poem even now. Otherwise, his books have curdled and wrinkled, yellowing with age as they were once yellow with youth. His plays, *Earnest* apart, constitute so much epigrammatic sardoodling. His verse is a joke. And if, as edited by Rupert Hart-Davis, the published collection of his correspondence resembles some marvellously absorbing and even haunting epistolary novel (and might have been given the title *Les Liaisons dangereuses* had it not already been taken), the maudlin *De Profundis*, which he addressed from prison to his alter id, the indefensible Bosie, cannot be read today without – to paraphrase Oscar himself on the death of Little Nell – shedding tears of uncontrollable laughter.

Yet there he still is, after all, Oscar Wilde, the household name par excellence. And again I ask, Why?

In response one might mention his courage and fundamental lovability. His soft bigness of build, both sluggish and sluglike, which was somehow, against all the odds, lovable in itself. His fabled generosity, rare in a wit and raconteur. (It's not by chance that, his own wit aside, he is also remembered for having publicly greeted another man's wit by commenting 'I wish I'd said that' – but who now remembers what it was Whistler said that prompted such humility and can anyone suppose that Whistler would have made the same disarming confession of impotence and frustration to Oscar if their roles had been reversed?) The fact, too, as Ellmann and others have pointed out, that the best of his paradoxes are unforgettable not simply because they are witty but because, and this is perhaps the paradox of paradoxes, they are *true*. Then there's the well-made, three-act perfection of the cautionary tale that his life was to become, with Oscar tempted by practically every sin in the calendar until, in the end, he permitted himself to be tempted by sheer Christian goodness. And one could cite at last his handiness as a perennial model against which subsequent, and comparable, artists may be measured. (Thus Joe Orton might be defined as the Oscar Wilde of platitudes rather than paradoxes, and one might even compare to Oscar and Bosie the monstrous ménage composed of Orton and his lover Kenneth Halliwell, except that in their case, unfortunately, it was Oscar who found himself in Bosie's body and Bosie in Oscar's.)

There is, though, one reason for his undiminished topicality that no one, I think, has ever commented upon, probably because it wouldn't be regarded as 'serious'. Which is that there seem to be quite a lot of people around – the dancer Lindsay Kemp, the novelist and performance artist Neil Bartlett, the 'self-invention' Quentin Crisp, but also a surprising number of complete unknowns, those private individuals treated by the arts, media and show business community as so many 'commoners' – who continue to ape Oscar's mannerisms, who imitate, however feebly, his wit, who even dress not unlike the way he dressed, who, in short, want to *be* Oscar Wilde – a man who died almost a century ago.

This is a phenomenon that is surely peculiar to Oscar. Widely admired though they may still be, no one any longer wants to 'be' Henry James or Thomas Hardy or Rudyard Kipling. Indeed, the only other English-language writer whose influence (on right-wing journalists, mainly: Richard Ingrams, Auberon Waugh, Charles Moore and that ilk) has just as radically telescoped the centuries dividing him from us is that emblematic embodiment of bull-headed common sense, the fogey's fogey, Dr Johnson. And perhaps what has made Oscar indispensable to many of us is that his wisdom, uniquely, is unencumbered by any of the more conventional, the more received, attributes of wisdom; that he offers a necessary counter-example to the kind of crude Johnsonian pragmatism which enjoys giving the world a choleric kick in the shins every so often to prove to it that it's there; and that he obliges us once and for all to choose between two diametrically opposed world-views, between (as he himself might have put it) Dr Johnson, who knew everything, and Oscar Wilde, who knew everything else.

Filming the unfilmable

What is there in common between, on the one hand, a unicorn and, on the other, the act of incest? Psychoanalytically speaking, who would dare to say? From the point of view of cinematic representation, though, there is at least this – that both of them belong to the category of the unfilmable.

For what exactly, in the spectator's eyes, is a unicorn on film (as, for example, in Ridley Scott's fantasy, *Legend*)? A horse with a plastic horn stuck to its brow. That's it. That's all there is to it. The basic problem of representational credibility which it poses is therefore not one of filmic artifice in itself (unicorns don't exist, of course, yet neither do werewolves or Martians or E. T.s, for whose illusory sakes most of us are nevertheless willing to suspend our collective disbelief) but the frustrating and anticlimactic ease with which such artifice has been engineered. Devising a plausible unicorn for a film necessitates none of the computerised sorcery of which the employees of George Lucas's Industrial Light and Magic are the currently unchallenged masters; neither an artisan's skill nor a poet's imagination need be called into play. And it's because of this *compulsory* absence of labour, in a medium in which, by definition, labour must not merely be applied but be seen to be applied, a medium for which virtually the only effects that count nowadays are special effects, that these beautiful and poetic but hopelessly uncomplicated beasts have always stubbornly declined to come alive on the screen.

As for incest, it would appear fated to remain, in the cinema as in life, the ultimate sexual heresy. Most varieties of deviant sexuality (male and female homosexuality, troilism, sadomasochism, bestiality) can be and have been represented by the cinema. Even if they are simulated, as almost always tends to be the case, the codes of narrative illusionism, when properly functioning, will end by recuperating any stray shreds of disbelief left unsuspended. In the way of 'incest', however, what have such (rare) cinematic treatments of the theme as Louis Malle's *Le Souffle au coeur* and Bernardo Bertolucci's *La Luna* had to offer? A simulated erotic relationship between an adolescent boy and a woman *old enough to be his mother* – which, although disquieting and, if you like, arousing as far as it goes, is not at all the same thing. Only Roger Vadim, by directing Jane Fonda to make googoo eyes at her brother Peter in his inept and meretricious episode of the portmanteau film *Spirits of the Dead*, could be said to have come close to breaching the taboo.

Another example of the unfilmable occurred to me a couple of weeks ago in Paris while watching Claude Chabrol's latest film, an adaptation of Henry Miller's *Quiet Days in Clichy*.

It is, as it happens, a total, ludicrous nullity, not, I'm afraid, the first such in its director's notoriously uneven filmography, but what it impressed upon me is that no one – save possibly Fellini in his version of the *Satyricon* – has ever succeeded in filming a plausible orgy. In the orgies that make up practically the entire running time of *Quiet Days in Clichy* (an irresistibly tempting title for any critic with a penchant for puns) a host of naked revellers writhe and swarm over one another like so much spaghetti bolognese, they do their pathetic utmost to look sybaritic and sex-crazed and they fail utterly, as so many have failed before them, to convince one that they are having even a reasonably nice time, let alone that they have been transported to some seventh hell of licentious carnality.

As usual, too, piled high and glistening in golden goblets, or else dangled above open, tongue-flicking mouths, is that ubiquitous prop, that inescapable signifier, of the orgy: the bunch of grapes.

But the classic instance of a subject which has always defied and will always defy cinematic treatment (a handful of documentaries apart) is the Final Solution. The day I understood, once and for all, that the concentration camps should never be fictionalised in film was the day I was conducted around a Hollywood studio, several years ago, and witnessed the obscene spectacle of bony, striped pyjama-clad extras from the television 'sitdram' (or situation drama) *Holocaust* tucking into a slap-up luncheon in the commissary. What revolted me was less the incongruity of such cadaverous creatures enjoying the same privileges after all as any other actors on the studio lot than my uneasy conviction that the conditions of the series's own fabrication must have mimicked, however faintly, those of the institutionalised horrors that it sought to depict. Thus these extras must have responded to very delicately worded advertisements in the Hollywood trade press (identifiably 'Jewish' types being especially prized); they would doubtless have had to strip for the casting director to prove that they were indeed as underfed and skeletally built as required; they would then have been herded off to have their heads shaved; and so on.

Such wilfully self-inflicted humiliations were infinitely less appalling than those portrayed in the series itself, but humiliations they were nevertheless. And I understood then that to endeavour to rate one film on the Holocaust as 'better' or 'less good' than another is comparable to assessing the more stylish of two lampshades made out of human skin.

The Flintstones

For anyone like myself still under the sway of the Puritan work ethic, for any workaholic, as I am, temperamentally incapable of going on the wagon, television, like sex, is not something to be indulged in during the afternoon. It's a pleasure to be taken exclusively in the evening, as in some households sex used to be (and may even now be) reserved for Saturday nights. The other day, however, having pulled a muscle in my back, I creakily manoeuvred my TV set to the foot of my bed, extended myself in front of it, braced myself for the upcoming shock to the system and switched on. The screen lit up just as though it *were* the evening, and what I happened upon was, of all things, *The Flintstones*.

I confess, though, that the shock I registered was not exactly of the type I had anticipated. Instead, it felt as though I had been ensnared in a time warp, whisked back, not to the cartoon's Stone Age setting, but to the Stone Age of my own life – to, in a word, my childhood. *The Flintstones* was one of the first cartoon series I can remember ever having watched on television, and my memories of its textures were so speedily refreshed that I found I was not only able to hum its idiotic theme tune with its no less idiotic catchphrase, 'Yabba-dabba-doo!', but also that I was blessed with apparently total recall as to the micro-narrative of its credit-title sequence: Fred and Wilma take in a Stone Age drive-in movie at which Fred is served a caveman rib of beef (presumably the Stone Age equivalent of a cheeseburger and French fries) of such a generous proportion that it causes their Stone Age automobile to capsize.

My initial response to what I was seeing was a purely nostalgic one, a luxuriantly regressive wallow in the snows (or shows) of yesteryear. Yet, being a critic, and therefore unwilling for too long to relinquish my self-appointed function as the public's food-taster, I set about scrutinising it with a more analytical eye and gradually found it to be – as is the case, no matter how outwardly trivial the context, with every work of art (a term I employ here in its descriptive rather than evaluative sense) – unexpectedly 'relevant'.

For anyone who is unfamiliar with, or has forgotten, its basic premise, *The Flintstones* (produced by William Hanna and Joseph Barbera, a team of animators, the creators of *Tom and Jerry*, celebrated in a splendid new coffee-table album) is a cartoon sitcom whose protagonists are a 'typical' Stone Age couple – Fred Flintstone, the sort of gruff, lovable bumbler endemic to the whole genre, and his irrepressibly long-suffering wife, Wilma – and their next-door neighbours, the Rubbles, Barney and Betty. The prototype is, self-evidently, *I Love Lucy* or *The Honeymooners*. But what is peculiar to this really rather peculiar programme is the amazingly little difference that being set in Stone Age suburbia makes to its plotlines. The Flintstones may be cave-persons, they nevertheless drive a Stone Age car, own a Stone Age TV set, dishwasher and refrigerator, and read a Stone Age daily newspaper (carved, as one might expect, on stone). And although, in the earliest episodes of the series, a lot of the humour would probably have derived from the comic potential of this kind of generalised anachronism, one eventually came to accept it as being just as much of a narrative given as the fact that Hamilton Burger, the state attorney in the old *Perry Mason* series, was never once allowed to win a case against his arch-opponent.

Now, every work of art is both functional (which is to say, it is designed to operate effectively on the level of its own discourse) and metaphorical (in that, whether limpidly or opaquely, it will as a rule reverberate on other, deeper levels). And it struck me as I watched it that *The Flintstones*, too, offered a startlingly precise metaphor for the current, calamitous state of this country's infrastructure after more than a decade of Thatcherite capitulation to market forces on a specifically, mythically American model. One has only to look around one in London to realise that, beyond all of contemporary capitalism's surface sheen, beyond the computers and cellular telephones, the aerials and squarials, the bar codes and junk mail, the credit cards and fax machines, the fast food outlets and hundred percent mortgages, beyond, in short, everything that was supposed to have put the 'Great' back into 'Great Britain', there continues to fester a dark, grubby, primitive Stone Age metropolis. Some of its inhabitants live in cardboard caves. Others, more fortunate, are nevertheless obliged to make a twice daily descent into vast, echoing and pee-smelling underground caverns whose walls are streaked with caveman grafitti. Still others make their perilous way through pitted thoroughfares strewn with the carcasses of fried chickens. And not a few of them, finally, just days after I watched *The Flintstones*, found themselves engaging in a pitched battle in protest against the imposition of a Stone Age poll tax.

And I thought of another work of filmic craft, a work of a rather more elevated standing, in which two separate time-frames are no less radically juxtaposed, Stanley Kubrick's *2001*, and the most celebrated jump-cut in the history of the cinema – when, in the film's prologue, a caveman hurls a bone high into the air only for the spectator to see it transformed, via a single cut, into a satellite in space. Metaphors are nicely reversible things, and perhaps what has been happening to Britain in the past decade is that the satellite has at last changed back into a bone.

Black and white in colour

Who remembers colorization? Because of how little one currently hears of the phenomenon, not to mention the fact that, as far as I am aware, no colorized film has ever been screened in this country (although the situation is doubtless already changing with satellite television), it has been slightly prematurely assumed that the issue is now a closed book; for once a won, not a lost, cause.

Such, however, is not at all the case. On American television colorized movies are quite regularly shown, viewers having conclusively opted for the cosmetised rather than the authorised version of cinema history; and the often vigorously voiced protests of the medium's most powerful luminaries (not just its 'artists') are beginning to sound like faintly desperate rearguard actions. The most recent test case was provided by Robert Wise's *The Haunting*, an admired supernatural thriller colorized by the Turner Entertainment Co. against the wishes of its director who had actually, back in 1963, had a prescient clause inserted in his contract ensuring (as he trusted) that his choice of black-and-white cinematography, already exceptional by the mid-sixties, be respected by the studio.

I ought perhaps to confess at once that I have never seen a colorized film, a fact which may appear to disqualify me from addressing the subject at all and the controversy surrounding it. Yet to be opposed to colorization one is not required to have been exposed to its effects. For the purist there can be no distinction made between 'well' and 'badly' colorized films: it's the principle, not the process, to which exception is taken.

Thus the polemic is an entirely false one. There is no possible justification for the vandalising of any film, however mediocre, save the exclusively mercenary one of 'giving the public what it wants', a public which has long been conditioned by television to dismiss black-and-white as a historical imperfection that will henceforth be repaired by the latest computer technology. For most members of that public a black-and-white film resembles nothing so much as a black-and-white television set; it's an embarrassing anachronism that they cannot wait to trade in. As no basis therefore exists for serious debate on the ethics of violating even undistinguished productions, what is there to be said on the matter beyond shrill sloganising of the 'Black-and-White is Beautiful' variety?

It might first be worth pointing out that, since black-and-white cinematography is coterminous with a fairly precise era of film history, colorization represents the real anachronism, an anachronism as indefensible as would be the engrafting of a belated soundtrack on to a silent classic. To be sure, in a strict chronological framework, the period of its pre-eminence is much less clearly demarcated than that of the silents, but it may be said to have extended approximately from the origins of the cinema itself to the mid-fifties and it continues to function as, at the very least, an infallible conductor of nostalgia (as in Woody Allen's *Zelig* and Martin Scorsese's *Raging Bull*).

In the second place, and transcending the more ephemeral manifestations of such nostalgia, there is a (somewhat whimsical) case to be made for black-and-white as an indelible period attribute, almost as a sociocultural state of mind. Would anyone understand what I meant if I proposed, for example, that Auden's verse and the thirties novels of Isherwood and Orwell were somehow 'in black-and-white'? Was it entirely incidental that Picasso, when painting *Guernica*, elected to resist the temptation of those brasher, more ingratiating hues at whose manipulation he was so brilliantly adept? Or that, on a more modest level of achievement, L. S. Lowry conjured up his bleak but chummy Northern landscapes principally in blacks, whites and eggshell greys? Or again, reverting to the cinema, that the thirties and forties witnessed the ascendancy of *film noir* thrillers in America and France and of the so-called *telefono bianco* comedies in Italy?

And, third, there is the fact that the cinema has in a sense already been colorized. When producers of TV commercials promote their products by employing Humphrey Bogart look-alikes, bogus Bogies, these simulacra are for obvious reasons almost invariably in colour whereas the actor's own films were of course mostly in black-and-white. That may appear a pedantically trivial point to raise, but it can be replicated a hundredfold and is symptomatic of how film, of late, has become increasingly *diffracted*. If fewer people are going to the cinema these days, it is because – through advertisements, books, posters, record sleeves and billboards, through the multiple reflecting and signifying surfaces of contemporary urban existence – the cinema is coming to them. For what is the 'cinema' now but Olive Oyl rag dolls and Betty Boop bars of soap, Tom Cruise pinups and Holsten commercials, sequels and prequels, remakes and (one day, I suppose) premakes? In the wilfully encouraged confusion of old and new, of good and bad, of film, television and video, the cinema is now less a specific art form than a *mythology*. And what, has been dismantled in the mythologising process is essentially its own history, whose exact chronological co-ordinates – of which black-and-white cinematography is by no means the least significant – no one any longer feels the need or the urge to respect.

The story of everybody

The notion of a game in which every player ends up a winner ought logically to belong among the paradoxes of Zen philosophers. Yet such a game actually does exist, even if the word 'game', an apt enough term for the mindless amusement it offers at a frivolous level, does not begin to do justice to its more global implications. Should you choose, however, not to explore these implications, it still offers an agreeably trivial pursuit for a languorous day at the beach, requiring not an ounce of skill, ingenuity or even chance.

Since one can call a game anything one pleases, this one could be called Uncle Silas or Tobermory or Jack-in-the-Middle (and another torpid pastime – just as trifling as, but trickier than, the one I'm about to describe – would be the coining of real names for imaginary games and the subsequent devising of real games to fit the imaginary names). For once, though, let us be boringly literal and call it Contacts.

The easiest way to explain how Contacts works is to cite a personal example. So: I am acquainted with a journalist from *Le Monde* who some years ago interviewed the novelist (and the then French Minister of Culture) André Malraux, who in his turn, if several years before that, had known Mao-tse-Tung in Peking. Which means that no more than two intermediaries, my journalist acquaintance and Malraux, stood between me and one of the most powerful men in the world. And if, in this particular instance, the time-frame is a trifle skewed, the idea that, accompanied by my friend from *Le Monde*, I could *just conceivably* have encountered Malraux in China and *just conceivably* have been introduced by him to Mao is not beyond – well, not completely beyond – the realm of possibility. Had I then, adjusting to my new high-powered self-image, used Mao as a further interlinking middleman, I would potentially have had access to everyone who was anyone on the geopolitical stage.

The principle of the game is therefore that each player propose a name, most congenially but not necessarily a famous one, and the others estimate how many such intermediaries it would take for them to make or have made contact with the individual named. And that is why no one really loses out. That is the democratic beauty of it all. If I, let's assume, am two contacts away from a certain celebrity, then, merely by virtue of playing opposite me, my adversaries simply add my own name as a third. In fact, so can anyone at all who knows me. Thus my late grandmother was just three contacts away from Mao-tse-Tung, a revelation I feel certain she would have taken in her stride. Her oldest and dearest friend, Mrs Bagent from two doors down, was only four. And Mrs Bagent's son-in-law, now a solicitor's clerk in Bath, is five (unless he should know a shorter route to Mao, one bypassing me altogether).

Naturally, it is of considerable help if you belong to a profession where bona fide access to the literati, glitterati and twitterati of the moment instantly opens up a conduit to those whose paths yours has not yet crossed. But even if you start without so clear an advantage, the truth is that, unless you are a member of one of the lost tribes of New Guinea, you will find yourself making contact with the brightest and the best of this world infinitely more rapidly than you would ever have believed possible.

That is what is ultimately so vertiginous about such a game. It demonstrates in a transparent manner a fundamental fact of civilisation – the intimately, almost incestuously intercommunicating nature of its demographical composition – that most of us would otherwise be tempted to dismiss as a theoretical paradox, a fallacious one at that, telling us nothing about the way we really live. In fact, it has been calculated – this is, incidentally, the meaning of the title of John Guare's play *Six Degrees of Separation* – that for anyone in the civilised world no more than half-a-dozen contacts are necessary to connect up with *anyone else*. (One should not of course be too scrupulous about what precisely constitutes a contact: for the purposes of the game at least, a casual handshake tends to be regarded as the permissible minimum of social interaction.) And if one proceeds from the reasonable assumption that there is no one in the world who knows absolutely no one else, the mathematical basis of the theory is relatively simple. Think of the number of people you have met in your lifetime, then of the number of people each of them is likely to have met, and so on; notwithstanding the fact that a lot of these contacts are bound to overlap from person to person, you will soon realise how remarkably few intermediate stages are needed to exhaust the world's vast but still finite kitty of humankind.

As with space, so with time: the vertical, as you might say, reserves just as many surprises as the horizontal. As a film critic, I once had the privilege of interviewing Lillian Gish, an actress as old as the cinema itself – indeed, a few giant redwoods aside, she is probably now the oldest living thing in Southern California. When a mere snip of ten (which is to say, in 1906) she *just conceivably* might have met and talked to a ninety-year-old woman (one therefore born in 1816) whose grandfather *just conceivably* might have thrilled her as an infant with a first-hand account of the French Revolution. Only three connections, then, separate me (yes, yes, hypothetically) from Danton and Robespierre.

I daresay that, once the instant of epiphany has passed, once one's fleeting conviction that everything is at last meaningful has evaporated, this apprehension of how snugly interconnected the human family turns out to be is actually quite futile, the sort of speculation that would prompt Mrs Bagent to say 'Makes you think, doesn't it?' and change the subject. Certainly, if I were asked just what it all proves, I would have to reply that I don't know – but I would add that there are some questions to which 'I don't know' happens to be the correct, 10-out-of-10, answer.

Brecht and the British

What is it with Brecht and the British? Brecht was, to be sure, many things the British inherently distrust, especially when they are combined in a single individual – he was, unforgivably, a German, an intellectual and a Marxist – but other dramatists have surmounted and survived comparably damning impediments. Brecht obliges his audiences to think for themselves – but so, their admirers would argue, do Ibsen and Shaw, Miller and Stoppard, whose works have never provoked anything like the same ingrained rancour and exasperation. Since the extraordinarily supple rhythms of Brecht's language cannot plausibly be translated into English, spectators must make the considerable imaginative leap of translating themselves into German – but then, similar claims might be made of Chekhov and Pirandello. So what is it with Brecht and the British?

I pose such a question because of another question, one that was posed, in the London *Evening Standard*, by its drama critic, Milton Shulman, in the opening paragraph of his review of Philip Prowse's current production of *Mother Courage* at the Mermaid. Schulman confesses smugly to a disgust with Brecht and all his works that dates back to the Berliner Ensemble's visit to London in 1956. What he wrote then, and is content to endorse now, is 'Not only have his homilies a musty ring of old-fashioned communist propaganda but they are laboriously etched out as if for an audience of illiterate peasants.' Reflect for a moment on those two words 'illiterate peasants'. For Shulman, of course, whose world seems circumscribed by Shaftesbury Avenue, and whose ideal theatre audience would be composed of upper middle-class and lower middlebrow readers of the *Evening Standard*, they are intended to be read as nothing more than an uncouth insult, whereas Brecht would certainly have regarded it as a triumph of democratic populism were part of his public actually to have been drawn from their ranks. But the question that Shulman poses is: 'Now that Marxism is discredited and in its death throes, how long can Bertolt Brecht survive?'

Naturally, the fact that every artist is shaped by a complex set of social, historical and political determinants means that the nature of his or her 'relevance' to any potential public will be modified as these determinants are modified, either by a gradualist process of evolution or else by some convulsive revolutionary spasm. Yet Chekhov's melancholy comedies have continued to hold the stage decades after the October Revolution that consigned to the dustbins of history the leisurely, affluent, feudal milieu in which they are set; and that Ibsen's plays are anchored in the rigidly bourgeois ideologies of nineteenth-century Norway has not prevented contemporary audiences (or critics) from being able to empathise with Nora and Hedda. So, again, what is it with Brecht and the British?

Shulman's own duckbilled platitudes on the subject need not detain us for very long. What is interesting, though, is that his obtuseness is 'transparent' in exactly the sense of the word as it was used by Barthes to describe *Mother Courage*. The specific greatness of the play (Barthes proposed) lies not in providing audiences with a textbook blueprint of the dramatist's perhaps too famous 'alienation technique' but rather in allowing them to understand the source of Mother Courage's subjugation to her oppressors by virtue of the fact that she herself never understands it. That is what he meant by 'transparency': 'Brecht alone, perhaps,' he wrote, 'has glimpsed the necessity, for socialist art, of always taking Man on the eve of Revolution, that is to say, alone, still blind, on the point of having his eyes opened to the revolutionary light by the "natural" excess of his wretchedness.' And he succinctly summed it up thus: 'To see someone who does not see is the best way to be intensely aware of *what* he does not see.'

So it is, too, with a critic like Milton Shulman. For Shulman the stage is a repository of eternal, unchanging and unchangeable values. If one were to venture a comparison, it would be less with an *altar* (which he would no doubt regard as too pretentious a metaphor, too suggestive of that aura of dramaturgical ritual with which he has as little truck as with Brecht's epic theatre) than perhaps a *bed*, a piece of furniture which has remained virtually unchanged since mankind first dropped out of the banana trees. We do almost everything in a more 'sophisticated' way than even our immediate forebears, but we still sleep on an unsophisticated horizontal couch and we still watch actors act on an unsophisticated raised platform. I myself would suggest, then, that what certain British critics so dislike about Brecht is not that he had radical ideas *in* the theatre but that he had radical ideas *about* the theatre, about its function and its future. (In this he differed from Ibsen, Shaw, Miller and Stoppard, none of whom saw any reason not to respect the apron stage's bedlike simplicity and purity.) He thereby compelled these critics to think long and hard about what the theatre is for and, by extension, about what theatre critics are for. So, as Milton Shulman trundles his review column, round and round, week after week, year after year, like Mother Courage trundling her cart around the stage of the Mermaid, it is precisely because of his chronic myopia that we are made the more intensely aware of the genius of Bertolt Brecht.

The smokers' secret society

On a hoarding just a few hundred yards or so from where I live there is what I consider to be an utterly revolutionary advertisement for Camel cigarettes. Filling the leftward half of this rectangular poster is the trademark ruminant itself, with facial features astonishingly like John Updike's as they might be reflected on the concave surface of a very large spoon, and the firm's slogan 'The Legend in Lights' (the last word of which my inner eye cannot help mentally correcting, *à l'américaine*, to 'Lites'); and on its rightward half is the rigorously and archaically unmetaphorical image of a half-open pack of Camels, its proferred alignment of cigarettes ascending sequentially from left to right like the pipes of a cathedral organ. It's the sheer banality of that image that seems to me a revisionist breakthrough, as though it were still thought possible, in a period when smokers are regarded as social outcasts, ostracised as self-willed untouchables, to use a pack of cigarettes to advertise a pack of cigarettes, its openness, moreover, connoting a candid, clubby ambience where it is the most natural yet also most sophisticated thing in the world (but what a yokel's word is 'sophisticated'!) to share a cigarette with a friend.

I should declare my interest at once: I myself am a smoker. Let me add, however, that I have never proselytised for my 'rights' as a free agent (the campaign currently being waged in public strikes me as wholly manipulative) and I am immediately prepared to stub out my cigarette at a sign of distaste from anyone, even a complete stranger, happening to be in my vicinity. Actually, there's nothing I wish more than to be capable of giving up and I have already tried and failed several times. What non-addicts fail to realise, alas, is that, when one *has* given up, the precise cigarette that one is desperately forcing oneself not to smoke is in a way the most tempting of all – which is to say, that first cigarette smoked after weeks or months or even years of self-deprivation and which, simply by virtue of the preceding abstinence, tastes better than any other.

Yet even if the most pressing incentive to quit smoking remains the danger to life and health, there's certainly a now widely held view that more recent converts to non-smoking have been influenced by the increasingly vocal resentment and displeasure which smokers tend to encounter pretty much everywhere. I wonder. For what public disapproval may also be doing is driving impenitents underground, engendering a belated *complicity* of addicts, a nationwide web of sociocultural dissidence held together by the kind of tribal honour that is usually claimed for thieves and spies. For the contemporary smoker there exist few more cherishable sights than that of *someone else smoking*, someone else pulling out his pack of Benson and Hedges or Silk Cut or Peter Stuyvesant and lighting up *first*. How does one convey to the non-smoker the delicious relief and reassurance that such a precedent-setter brings us, the exchange of knowing half-smiles that follows, the palpable sense of community, of a shared and secret predilection? Although he (that is, the more devil-may-care smoker) may initially have struck one as rather chilly or standoffish or boring or whatever, suddenly he seems an agreeable enough fellow after all, he has a way with him that one just can't help warming to, it only goes to show that one really shouldn't make snap judgments about people. And in a climate in which social pressures will continue to bear on smokers either to pamper their filthy cravings in hermetically sealed intimacy or desist from them altogether, this sense of an occult fraternity of misunderstood martyrs will no doubt flourish.

But to return to advertising: much as I abominate it in general, abominate the mercantile garrulity of a culture whose principal ambition has become that of selling us something, I own to being constantly amazed by the near-supernatural ingenuity of the advertising profession. For what made the Camel advertisement so revolutionary was of course the fact that most of the other tobacco companies now seem determined actually to undermine what one had always supposed to be the point, the *raison d'être*, of a promotional campaign – which is to publicise a product, to render its existence and, by extension, its merits *public*. Thus the Silk Cut ads (amusingly analysed by David Lodge in a passage of *Nice Work*) have opted for a series of textless variations on the ideas of 'silk' and 'cutting', culminating, recently, in the image of an *uncut* purple silk shower curtain which will only make sense to those who have seen Hitchcock's *Psycho*. (But then, who hasn't?) Benson and Hedges relies exclusively for its selling point on the precise shade of gold familiar from its cigarette packets (gold deckchairs blown away on a seaside promenade, gold stubble from a shaver's chin) with nary a cigarette in sight. And one poster I recall was so extraordinarily enigmatic that the only indication, as far I could make out, of the precise nature of the product being publicised – its only signifier, in other words – was, by a perverse paradox, the Surgeon-General's health warning.

What are these advertisements up to? Basically, I suggest, they are alerting the initiated to the fact that they are not alone; that, if they are indeed outcasts, well then, so were the Early Christians; and that, like the Early Christians, if they remain united, they must in the end prevail. The tobacco companies are, in short, elevating to a national plane the cryptic complicity which I mention above and which many an addicted smoker may eventually find as painful to give up as the cigarettes themselves.

A letter to the times

Of late I have grown increasingly alert to one of those great and simple truths of life of which everyone is doubtless aware but which no one ever seems prepared to acknowledge. I mean the fact that all the pious bromides, the homilies handed down from generation to generation, with which I had my ears bent back by my elders when I was an adolescent – that I would become more conservative with age, that my more radical opinions would be gradually smoothed out with experience, that my youthful passions would eventually come to strike my chastened older self as so many juvenile fatuities – bromides that I dismissed as reflecting a complete misreading of what I fancied was in its way a rather unique personality, my own – all of them, I say, have turned out to be absolutely, literally true. To my very great astonishment, an astonishment quite untempered by regret for my own vanished youth, I now find myself contemplating 'the younger generation', as well as the world in which it lives and thrives, with precisely the same contempt with which my predecessors contemplated me.

These reflections were occasioned – perhaps 'confirmed' would be the more fitting term – by reading, in a recent issue of the *Sunday Correspondent*, a superb piece by the novelist Justin Cartwright on the London of the nineteen-nineties and, by extension, on the debased and debasing culture which has been shaping its profile over the last few years.

What I most immediately responded to was his vivid word-portrait of the capital: a city from within whose inner confines it would currently be impossible to effect a complete 360° rotation without being confronted, from one angle or another, by an extended enclave of scaffolding and tarpaulin, as though the West End had become the object of some monstrous 'wrapping' project by the conceptualist sculptor Christo; a city with so many skips edging any given street as to cause it, in the sunshine, to resemble nothing so much as an animated stretch of the Suez Canal; a yobbish city in which there are just too many Colin Welland and Jim Davidson lookalikes for comfort (everyone knows what 'xenophobia' means, but does a word exist to define a fear of one's compatriots?); a thuggish dump of a metropolis in which the litterati far outnumber the literati and the general street chat can be reduced in the passer-by's ear (as with the regular thump-thump-thump of a bass beat that is all that is left of rock music when heard from two floors down) to the rhythmic pulse of the word 'fuck'.

In the larger context, however, Cartwright's conclusions helped to articulate for me my own alienation from contemporary British culture (in the least parochial sense of the word) and its fundamental *obscenity*.

The word 'obscene' means, in fact, 'off-stage', and it was first employed to describe those paroxysmal moments of crisis which, in both classical Greek and neoclassical French tragedies, had to be concealed from view because they were considered too appalling to be exposed to the eyes of the public. Etymologically speaking, then, by virtue of the unashamed relish with which it flaunts its protagonists' passions and pains, melodrama is an 'obscene' form; and, on much the same basis, it may be claimed that we are living in an obscene society, a society for which the endless subjection of London's pavements and roads to gruesome open-heart surgery, the endless disinterring of its surfaces to discover what horrors might be lurking underneath, offers the perfect metaphor.

It's a society in which, if you have made it, if you are not one of life's losers (there are no 'victims' of society any longer, only losers), virtually anything is permitted, virtually anything goes. It's a society in which the sort of prejudice and corruption that would in a more 'classical', less 'melodramatic' phase of our cultural history certainly have existed but remained off-stage is now almost gleefully paraded before us. It's a society in which, to paraphrase Leona Helmsley, morals are for little people. It's a society in which, to cite only the most recent and flagrant example, Nicholas Ridley, a cabinet minister, one of the Prime Minister's most intimate allies, blithely lets himself go on record in the *Spectator* spouting the crassest prejudices of the tabloid press on the subject of German reunification. It's a society in which David Steel, although condemning Ridley's outburst, can nevertheless defend him as an engaging and disarming eccentric. (Whenever I hear the word 'disarming' I reach for my revolver.) It's a society in which the term 'kraut' is now widely accepted in print with a half-amused, oh-well-what-can-one-say indulgence. It's a society in which one tabloid newspaper or another reported that 94% of its readers actually came out in support of Ridley's blimpish xenophobia. (It scarcely matters which tabloid. Trying to distinguish between the *Sun*, the *Star* and the *Mirror* would be like poking into a blocked-up toilet and trying to figure out which turd came from which backside.) And, to forestall any objection that he was, after all, compelled to resign, I would suggest that what his repulsive interview really demonstrated is just how far you have to go these days before you will be called to account.

In my day (but I admit that I may be romancing the past) such licence was simply not conceivable. And what was my day? The sixties, the derided, the now universally maligned and mocked sixties. Yet, if that quintessential sixties word 'permissive' means anything, it must surely refer to a society in which practically anything is permitted, in which no opinion, no prejudice will be regarded as too obscene to be aired in public. In short, the true permissive society is the one we are living in now.

Lookalikes

Other people's lavatories, I find, are curious, rather off-putting places and they possess two immutable properties. One, without exception, the flush will fail to work the first time I try to use it, obliging me to jerk it down more and more frantically as it meets with less and less resistance. (In like manner, if ever I borrow a friend's apartment, for some mysterious reason the front door key always, *but always*, has to be jiggled this way and that before it will properly turn in the lock.) Two, I can usually depend upon finding, at a handy arm's length, a little shelf of reading matter, among which there is guaranteed to be one or several books published under the imprint of *Private Eye*.

Lavatories, like dentist's waiting-rooms, have begun to generate something of a literary subculture of their own (a book of mine was once commended by the London listings magazine *City Limits* as offering '*louche* loo reading'), but what concerns me is less the phenomenon in general than one *Private Eye* publication in particular that I recently chanced to pick up while spending a penny in a friend's weekend cottage. *The Eye Spy Lookalike Book* is a compendium of those jokey items regularly published on its letters page (like every other feature in *Private Eye*, the joke is a relentlessly 'running' one) in which two photographs of faces bearing an unexpected resemblance to each other are printed side by side with, underneath, a poker-faced note suggesting that the individuals in question might be related. Naturally, the more incongruous these face-sakes are, the funnier the joke: thus Arthur Scargill and Rossini; Terry-Thomas and General Zia of Pakistan; 'Hilda Ogden' (of *Coronation Street*) and Simone de Beauvoir; and, my own all-time favourite, Doris Lessing and Geronimo.

What is the precise nature of the pleasure we take in such juxtapositions? In the first instance, surely, there is the pleasure of the *rhyme*. These faces rhyme with one another just as do the last two words of a verse couplet, and their confrontation on the page instils in us the same slight sense of wonder that might be prompted by some ingenious phonetic correspondence. (What strikes us as miraculous in the coining of a rhyme, as in the composing of a memorable melody, is our feeling that both rhyme and melody are already 'out there', just waiting to be plucked from the air; that their existence antedates that of the poet or composer, who have been blessed with good fortune rather than talent in capturing them.) Moreover, the very best of the Lookalikes are the least evident ones, those concerning which we require photographic evidence to be convinced that there exists a resemblance at all – Ken Dodd and Shirley Williams, George Michael and Desperate Dan, Malcolm Muggeridge and the Duchess of Kent – and they ought therefore to be equated not so much with traditional poetic rhymes as with those of song lyrics. To draw together out of nowhere two such ostensibly dissimilar physiognomies as those of Mick Jagger and Anita Loos and photographically 'alliterate' them is not so very different from what the lyricist Lorenz Hart did when he rhymed 'I'll go to Hell for ya' with 'Or Philadelphia' in the song 'Any Old Place With You'. The charm of both of these rhymes, the verbal and the photographic, is one that no truly serious poet or photographer would ever endeavour to induce. One is pleasurably conscious of a sense of contrivance indulged in for its own sake, of words and faces rhyming for the first and probably only time in their existence.

But there is also the pleasure to be derived from a collision of cultural associations. Most of the names cited first in the couplings above belong in the field of popular culture, the latter group in that of high culture, and this tends to be the rule of the book. There is, then, a wilfully debunking element to the joke. If Rossini suddenly seems to look a lot like Arthur Scargill, the effect on the reader is not so much to 'elevate' Scargill as to invest poor Rossini's features with a hitherto undetected coarseness and vulgarity; and the giddiness of which one might have been no more than half-aware in Shirley Williams's personality is brought into startling focus when her face is juxtaposed with Ken Dodd's.

So the joke can perhaps be interpreted most fruitfully as a miniaturised form of parody and even satire. (It functions in much the same way as a new book from Faber, *Unauthorised Versions*, whose editor – Kenneth Baker, as it happens – has juxtaposed a collection of classic poems and their own parodies.) To see 'Hilda Ogden' and Simone de Beauvoir twinned in this fashion is to have instantly exposed the latter's grotesque pretensions to populist feminism (the housewife's scrubbed countenance, the washerwoman's dishcloth turban, and so on). Nothing could more neatly puncture the modish absurdity of George Michael's designer stubble than the cactussy bristles of Desperate Dan's off-the-peg chin. And the strangely plausible resemblance between two Davids, Owen and Bowie (the same nonchalantly tousled hair, the same studied moue of rock star insolence), helps one to understand, no doubt glibly, why the former was so successful a politician and why, too, that success was ultimately so superficial.

'I wonder if they are by any chance related?' reads the standard accompanying query in *Private Eye*. Well, yes, since you ask, they are; but the relationship is sometimes a more subtle and revealing one than the magazine itself possibly realises.

One sweats, the other doesn't

Should you wish to interpret the dreams that America dreams, you need look no further than its cinema, since no other cinema in the world has offered as sensitive a diagnosis of a national psychology at any given point of its history. And should you wish to take the full measure of the American cinema, a cinema activated primarily by action and violence, you would be well advised to study its images of invulnerability.

During the summer of 1990, when the Hollywood studios levelled all their biggest guns at the rest of the world, the ultimate and, one is almost tempted to say, *terminal* image of invulnerability was indisputably Arnold Schwarzenegger – not merely the actor himself or the film, *Total Recall*, in which he was featured but the whole physico-ideological ideal of which he constitutes the most exemplary specimen. (Schwarzenegger is as top-heavy with ideology as he is with physicality.) But perhaps 'terminal' is too definitive a term for a quality – invulnerability – that is, paradoxically, in constant evolution. To a casual eye Schwarzenegger may now seem the *ne plus ultra* of physical indestructibility. Yet, only a few years ago, so did Sylvester Stallone, who currently cuts an almost risibly outmoded and unrepresentative figure (and has in consequence sought to reanimate a faltering career by transferring his allegiance to comedy).

What is it, then, that differentiates one from the other and also in what sense can the latter claim to represent an 'advance' on the former?

The difference, essentially, is that Stallone sweats and Schwarzenegger doesn't. As both Rambo and Rocky, his twin trademark roles, Stallone was positively lathered in sweat. He perspired with the professional facility with which certain maudlin actresses are capable of weeping on cue: hardly less excessive than his body's pectoral development was the sheer volume and abundance of the natural fluids that it secreted. And if he sweated it meant that he had an inside, he was flesh and bones, pores and ducts, kidneys and bowels. He was indestructible; but he was also, fatally, human. Nowadays, however, sweating has become as much of a gaffe for a superhero as farting, say, is for the rest of us. Which is why Schwarzenegger, for his part, is *literally* indestructible, which is to say, literally superhuman, which is in its turn to say, inhuman. In *Total Recall* he is pure surface, pure simulacrum, wholly bereft of anything as squishy and shameful as an 'inside'. His (tangential) relation to ordinary humankind is a primarily metaphoric one, as in the curious scene in which he confounds his adversaries by hologrammatically replicating himself. In an earlier film, moreover, *The Terminator*, the film that made him the most popular, the most 'bankable', star in the world, he was actually cast as a cyborg, a preprogrammed contraption that like an automobile could be 'dented' but never 'hurt'. When an accident somehow did occur, all he had to do was unscrew the impaired limb and reset the relevant mechanism. His soul, insofar as he might be said to have possessed one, was nothing more than the software of his existence. And if, about two-thirds of the way into both films, he found himself obliged after all to display a modicum of vulnerability – usually for no other purpose than that of keeping the plot awhir – his public, although as obscurely resentful of this momentary lapse as children are impatient with 'lovey-dovey' scenes in adventure movies, probably realised full well that it was merely a device of narrative self-preservation.

The metallic spectre of Schwarzenegger equally haunts *Robocop* and its new sequel, *Robocop II*, which is to be released here in a week or two. (It's one of the ironies of the contemporary American cinema that these films, whose very subject-matter is the electronic cloning of humanity, have themselves become part of a delirious, theoretically inexhaustible process of reduplication.) Both of them, significantly, are set in Detroit, the cradle of industrial mass production. As one of Robocop's inventors helpfully explains to a sceptical police officer, 'He doesn't have a name, he has a program. He's product.' *He's product.* Dehumanisation, previously understood as a totally pejorative concept, has now been transformed into a positive quality: clearly, for a cinema in thrall to special effects there can be no hero more symptomatic and more sympathetic than one who is himself a special effect. Within the context of the genre, we have thus arrived at the stage of what might be called *mineral* science-fiction, as distinct from the *animal* (*Gremlins*, for example) and *vegetable* (*Alien*) varieties. For the world in which Schwarzenegger moves *is* a primarily metallic one, an airless, sunless, claustrophobic, neon-lit moon, whose sole inkling of genuinely human imperfection among the futuristic tower blocks is a spoor of litter, that emblem and excrement of decadent consumerism.

Aesthetically speaking, there isn't one of these films – *The Terminator, Total Recall, Robocop I* and *II* – that is not repellent to the last degree and does not bear disturbing witness to the insidious Nazification of a minor but often amusing genre of the American cinema. Their appeal would seem to be based on an unholy compound of Fascism, fashion and fascination, and the fact that the heroes can be distinguished from the villains by being *slightly* less Fascistic in their methods can scarcely be regarded as a cause for admiring their 'radicalism', as Judith Williamson did in a recent, extraordinarily foolish and irresponsible *Guardian* article. But they do offer, as I say, images of a terminal America, a phantasmagoric projection into the very near future of anxieties that, although half-repressed, remain all too present.

And, while we are on the subject of superheroes, it might just be worth reminding Hollywood that what gave the ancestor of them all, Superman, his true strength and humanity was precisely the Kryptonite that debilitated him.

Bilko

Am I alone in finding something perversely frustrating about the endlessly repeated screenings of the *Bilko* show on television, a show I nevertheless adore and of which I cannot conceive of ever tiring? In actual, paradoxical fact, what is frustrated by its almost perennial recurrence in the schedules is *my longing to be nostalgic about it*. For oh, the delicious frisson of nostalgia I would now be experiencing had the series become merely one of television's more pleasantly blurry memories! With what wistful relish would I endeavour to recollect the very best of its plots! (For what it's worth, my own absolute favourite has always been the episode in which Bilko, beaten at poker for the first time in his life by the gormless mess cook Rupert Ritzig, subsides into so terminal a state of apathy that to every enquiry addressed to him he can only reply, in a voice of infinite weariness, 'I don't know, I just don't know . . .'). How I would enjoy swapping memories with my fellow Bilkophiles, swapping memories but also simply swapping names – Paparelli! Henshawe! Zimmerman! Fender! Dear, bumbling, fumbling old Colonel Hall! And, of course, last but not least (not least precisely because, in the pecking order of the Fort Baxter motor pool, he invariably *was* last), Doberman, the immortal slob!

Is it possible to be nostalgic about a phenomenon that happens to be still current? Is it possible to be nostalgic about the present? I pose the question because, whenever I watch *Bilko*, which I do with a positively *religious* fervour and fidelity, I find myself imbued with sentiments of love and forbearance towards it such as would be unimaginable with any equivalent programme, British or American, still being screened on television – such, indeed, as only the tenderising patina of the recent past is ever supposed to inspire.

This 'nostalgia' of mine is of course not altogether inexplicable, since the series does actually date from the fifties, as evidenced by its flatly lit black-and-white photography, its now unacceptably high incidence of fluffed lines of dialogue (Paul Ford, the show's Colonel Hall, being a notable if adorable offender), its unashamed, poignantly naïve and slavishly stereotyped deployment of musical clichés on the soundtrack to underscore some comical little plot point ('wah-wa-a-aah'), the unvaryingly breezy *envoi* with which each of its episodes signs off ('Also starring in tonight's show were . . .') and, above all, the bizarrely dated drabness of its army barracks setting, which, when viewed today, appears to be almost flaunting its miserabilism in just the way *Dallas* and *Dynasty* used to flaunt their gaudy affluence.

The crux of the matter, however, is that not only has a 'professional' like myself failed to retain over the years most of the actors' names (as distinct from the characters', which I believe I shall remember to my dying day) but that these actors seem *never* to turn up in any other TV show or film. It is true that before discovering his authentic and definitive vocation on television Phil Silvers himself was a fairly minor movie star in the forties and fifties (often cast as the hero's ebullient 'best friend' responsible for a climactic reconciliation with some temporarily estranged sweetheart); Paul Ford's is a name and face not unknown to film buffs; and Joe E. Ross ('Ritzig') also co-starred in another comedy show of the period, *Car 54, Where Are You?* But the members of the platoon? How startled I would be if Paparelli, for example, the rubbery-mouthed one incapable of keeping a secret, or peaky-faced Zimmerman, of the Tintin tuft of upswung hair, or that goggle-eyed, bespectacled and weirdly Oriental-looking one at the back, who is practically never allotted a line of dialogue and whose precise identity invariably escapes me, were to have materialised in some glossy Technicolor comedy of the fifties with Rock Hudson and Doris Day or some paranoid cold war thriller of the early sixties. It's almost as though the communal experience of the *Bilko* show had been so very special, so indelible, they simply could not bring themselves to besmirch its sacred memory by seeking subsequent employment elsewhere.

That, I realise, is just a sentimental fantasy. A far likelier explanation for their utter disappearance from circulation is that their lengthy and exclusive association with the series had rendered them all but unemployable. But such a wilful self-delusion only reinforces for me what I perceive as the show's *Utopian* essence, the sense I have of an exotic and hermetic microcosm sealed off from the rest of television, past and present, sealed off from that garrulous intertextuality that has soap-opera stars discussing their fictional selves on chat shows, weathermen being interviewed by Terry Wogan and 'the real' Edwina Currie (whoever she might be) making a coy guest appearance in a satirical drama on the gutter press.

And, ultimately, the series's Utopianism makes me think of another artist of whose work and world it has obscurely reminded me since I first started to watch it in my adolescence: P. G. Wodehouse. For me at least, Phil Silvers's Bilko is entirely worthy of comparison with Jeeves; the motor pool platoon with the chinless sybarites of the Drones Club; and Fort Baxter with that halcyon haven that has always been Blandings Castle.

So what would become of me if the BBC were at long last to decide to drop the series, once and for all, from its schedules? I don't know, I just don't know . . .

Kit & Port & Henry & June

Possibly because I was for several years an expatriate myself, I have long felt a distaste for what I might term *expatriate fictions*. By that I mean those novels (but also films), usually Anglo-American in origin, which were written and set mostly in the interwar period and whose narratives centred upon some raffish, inevitably 'artistic' English or Americans at large in a few plum localities of codified exotica. Paris was undoubtedly the genre's *locus classicus*, a Paris that during the twenties and thirties became for many an abbreviation for 'Paradise', but Berlin, Pamplona, Taormina, Capri, Tangier and the Côte d'Azur were other favoured watering holes.

Before attempting to examine what might be specific to the genre, however, two crucial distinctions have to be made. In the first place, not every novel written by an expatriate is necessarily an expatriate fiction: it was while he was based in Trieste and Paris, after all, that Joyce conjured up the Dublin of *Ulysses*; likewise, most of what Gertrude Stein wrote in her fabled apartment in the rue de Fleurus was 'set' (if that's really the word I'm looking for) in the United States. In the second place, expatriate fictions should never be equated with fictions of exile: the ideologies of exile and expatriation are almost always mutually exclusive.

The exasperation prompted in me by these works – the feeling I have that it's in *The Sun Also Rises*, a tersely written but paradoxically also rambling novel of the expatriate experience, that one finds Hemingway at his long-winded worst; that Fitzgerald's Dick and Nicole Diver from *Tender Is the Night* are in the reading as excruciatingly self-obsessed as Scott and Zelda themselves were reputed to have been in life – was recently reinforced by screenings of two new films, adaptations of Paul Bowles's *The Sheltering Sky* and Anaïs Nin's *Henry and June*, directed respectively by Bernardo Bertolucci and Philip Kaufman and due to be shown, both of them, at the current London Film Festival.

I intend here to concentrate on *The Sheltering Sky* since, Bertolucci being a considerably more accomplished filmmaker than Kaufman, it is much the superior film of the two. Yet, like Kaufman's, it suffers from a set of cultural assumptions that bedevil all expatriate fictions, especially in the cinema.

It opens, in the immediate wake of the Second World War, with the arrival in Morocco of its American hero and heroine, Kit and Port Moresby (played by Debra Winger and John Malkovich), with a charming if feckless socialite acquaintance, Tunner (Campbell Scott), in amiable tow. Bowles himself, an elderly, jaded exquisite carved out of bone, observes the rowdy progress of his own creations from the refuge of a café table. And, as it has been filtered through Vittorio Storaro's burnished cinematography, the Tangier at which they have docked, and which proves to be the portal to their descent into Hell, is a phantasmagoria of a thousand-and-one nightmares where forbidden fruit is openly bought and sold in the market-place.

So far, so good. The basic problem, though, is that Bowles's novel is now widely acknowledged as a minor classic of contemporary American literature. Widely acknowledged, too, is the fact that its principals are closely founded on the author himself and his wife Jane. Bertolucci knows that. The film knows that. It knows as well that we, as literate and informed spectators (the only kind of spectators such a film is ever likely to attract), will therefore assume, without having to be told, that Kit and Port are individuals as inherently glamorous and fascinating as their models. Consequently, it never for an instant troubles to *render* them glamorous and fascinating.

It's as though, as his sole nod in the direction of creating real characters, Bertolucci had had an enormous placard erected on the set of his film which read: 'Be sophisticated!' These cosmopolitan darlings of his know the palms of Morocco better than they know those of their own hands – even better, the implication would appear to be, than the poor, benighted locals themselves. They do 'crazy, wonderful things' like making love in the desert, on the very rim of nothingness, or blithely swallowing weevil-infested soup in some insalubrious horror of a restaurant while the gauche Tunner (whose presence is required in the narrative for no other reason than to set the cosmopolitanism of his companions, their devil-may-care worldliness, to maximum advantage) looks on in disgust. 'Oh Tunner,' squeals Kit at one point, 'stop trying to be interesting. On you it looks terrible.' On Kit herself, naturally, it looks great. Except, again, that Bertolucci makes no attempt to articulate the 'interest' she might be generating. Like so much else in *The Sheltering Sky*, it's a given which has been preprogrammed into the film. Jane Bowles, as we all know, *was* interesting, therefore Kit must be, too.

It's equally a given of the genre that, like the prettified Left Bank Paris of *Henry and June*, Morocco itself should forfeit the autonomous cultural and geographical existence that it possessed to become merely the arena in which the pyschodrama of Kit and Port is to be played out. Comparing tourism and travel (a fatal sign of the bogus), Port defines a tourist as 'the kind of person who wants to go home the day after he arrives'. (Port, of course, is a born traveller, as his name none too subtly intimates.) Yet one could just as well define a traveller – a traveller, that is, in the expatriate mould – as someone for whom every journey is primarily an 'inner journey', a 'voyage towards self-discovery and self-understanding', etc., etc. And I think: Tourists may often be crass and philistine, yet they can still claim the modest but not ignoble ambition of wishing to see, and learn something about, the countries they visit. For expatriates, at least as represented in fiction and film, travel tends to broaden not the mind but the ego.

Liff, death and the whole damn thing

There have always existed works of literature and art whose latent implications far outweigh their overt, often relatively humble intentions; others of which precisely the reverse is true, in that (to employ a coyly convoluted metaphor) the cheque of their declared intention bounces for want of sufficient funds in the great central bank of subject-matter. Recently, examples of both have happened to come my way.

In the former category I would place a little book which I received as a Christmas gift, Douglas Adams's and John Lloyd's *The Deeper Meaning of Liff* (a revised and expanded edition of their earlier *Meaning of Liff*), published by Pan as a droll self-styled 'dictionary of things that there aren't any words for yet'. Five randomly selected entries should give the reader a fairly accurate notion of what the authors are up to. (The proposed 'neologisms' themselves are the names of towns and villages 'which spend their time doing nothing but loafing about on signposts pointing at places.)

Lindisfarne (adj.) Descriptive of the pleasant smell of an empty biscuit tin. *Pimperne* (n.) One of those rubber nodules found on the underneath side of a lavatory seat. *Soller* (vb.) To break something in two while testing if you glued it together properly. *Wartnaby* (n.) Something you only discover about somebody the first time they take their clothes off in front of you. *Wasp Green* (adj.) The paint in the catalogue which is quite obviously yellow.

There are lots of other examples that are perhaps more conspicuously giggle-inducing ('*Waccamaw*: An exotic Brazilian bird which makes its home in the audiences of BBC Light Entertainment radio shows and screeches when it hears the word "bottom" '), some of them, indeed too many of them, scatological in nature, but I chose those five because they best illustrate what I believe is the book's real source of interest, as distinct from its humour. The peculiar pleasure of *Liff* is that of seeing in print – without any judgment being passed by the writers or required of their readers – an inventory of experiences that are uncannily familiar to us all but that 'do not deserve' to be in print. Or, perhaps I should say, that 'do not deserve' to form the unique subject-matter of a book (rather than a newspaper or magazine article), a book, moreover, signed by writers of considerable reputation (rather than by mere journalists). It is the pleasure of having to focus our attention for once on the kind of minutiae that novelists, dramatists, painters and filmmakers have traditionally excommunicated from their 'vision' but that nevertheless constitute the shared connective tissue, the frequently curious and charming trivia, of our lives.

At the risk of ruining the joke altogether, I would even go so far as to claim that the book not only reveals the astonishing number of things in the world which have never been named (if many of those cited by Adams and Lloyd are consciously facetious, several really ought to have names: 'the feeling', for example, 'of silver paper against your fillings') but also conveys an intimation of a humble yet obscure truth about language and literature. Which is that fiction may be generated just as powerfully by an absence as by a proliferation of words. Cocteau somewhere remarks that if there existed a word for 'the sort of love that causes a woman to feel that . . .' or 'the sort of jealousy that causes a man to believe that . . .', then the entirety of *A la Recherche du temps perdu* could be distilled in a compact five hundred pages. And it's possible to argue that the page-by-page articulation of virtually all fiction derives from a process whereby the writer, confronted with the absence of a single word to define some complex psychological state, is obliged to have recourse to a cluster of words, many of which in their turn require other word-clusters before they too can be satisfactorily pinned down, and so on . . . if not exactly *ad infinitum*, then at least to the point at which the novel is complete.

The Deeper Meaning of Liff is therefore one of those agreeably serendipitous works whose unpretentious public ambition (to make the reader laugh) conceals . . . well, a deeper meaning. As an example of the exact opposite, consider the exhibition about to open at the Museum of Modern Art in Oxford, of Steve Pyke's photographs of philosophers (Chomsky, Isaiah Berlin, etc.), a spread of which was featured in one of the very last issues of the *Sunday Correspondent*. Without prejudging the exhibition itself, which I have not seen, and setting aside the technical quality of the photographs, I do feel that there's a basic question to be asked here: to wit, what is the point of photographing a philosopher? Writers can be photographed writing (or pretending to write), painters painting and film directors pointing their index fingers, but a philosopher's vocation is after all to *think*, which is a wholly internalised activity, one that would appear to be inaccessible to photographic representation. Yet it was indeed Pyke's stated intention to communicate pure cerebrality as an image, as a *spectacle*. As he put it to the *Correspondent* interviewer: 'Perhaps by photographing these "thinkers" I hope to open some doors, open eyes, open minds.' And the interviewer, Robin Gibson, seems to think he did:

'These photographs map some of the most extraordinary minds of our time and, like philosophical questions, repay prolonged acquaintance.'

So does this gallery of intense, unsmiling, starkly highlighted faces, this collection of piercing eyes, bulging foreheads and beetle-browed strain (almost as though some revolutionary new concept were actually being formulated during the photographic session) really suggest febrile intellectual activity? Possibly so. More incongruously, it suggests to me something else as well, something a trifle less rarefied. I intend no disrespect to the philosophers themselves; but, looking at these photographs, I could not help thinking of the most famous of all artistic representations of the intellect at work, Rodin's *The Thinker*, and of the fact that it has traditionally prompted sniggers as a comically vivid lavatorial image.

Andy Hardy grows up

Culturally speaking, children are, as they say, in the air. During Christmas week BBC2 screened half-a-dozen five minute filmlets bearing the overall title of *How Are the Kids?* and shot by directors as disparate as Jerry Lewis, Jean-Luc Godard and the late Lino Brocka. The Barbican is about to launch its crosscultural 'Childhood' cycle, with productions of operas both for and about children, most notably *Higglety Pigglety Pop!* by Oliver Knussen and *Anne Frank* by the American conductor Michael Tilson Thomas; there are also concerts programmed around the theme of childhood, exhibitions of the work of Tenniel and Maurice Sendak, and a season of films 'looking at the world from the point of view of children themselves'. And Channel 4 has had a wholly unanticipated success with its recent Saturday-morning screenings of the nineteen-forties *Andy Hardy* series (for which Metro-Goldwyn-Mayer received an honorary Oscar 'for its achievement in representing the American Way of Life'). It was shown in its sixteen-episode entirety, including the belated 1958 epilogue, *Andy Hardy Comes Home*, in which Andy has grown up and become a family man himself.

In actual fact, as played by Mickey Rooney, Andy Hardy was not a child at all but a teenager. However, in view of his rather improbably respectful relationship with his father the Judge (a sanctimonious *paterfamilias* invested with, under the circumstances, quite amazing humour and humanity by Lewis Stone), his obsession with 'kissing' and apparently chronic obliviousness of the fact that that normally tends to be the first, not the last, word on romantic encounters with the opposite sex, and the boyishly falsetto 'Whoo-whoo-whoop!' with which he would bring almost all of the films to an end, the behavioural patterns that he displayed have become, in the intervening half-century, those of a pre- rather than post-pubescent youth. (And even then there can't be too many pre-pubescent youths around these days as relentlessly nice and innocent as he.)

That in itself lent the series interest simply as a touching document of the period – a document, one should add, less of realistic adolescent conduct than of parental wish-fulfilment fantasies. Yet, assuming that one managed not to gag on their homespun moralising, the experience of watching these films was a suprisingly complex one.

Much in evidence, to start with, was the perverse charm possessed by many of the least plausible books and films about children, books and films that are scarcely less absurd about the world of childhood than the eight-year-old Daisy Ashford's *The Young Visiters* was about that of grown-ups – scarcely less absurd yet in their way scarcely less entrancing. There was, too, the fairly irresistible nostalgia (by no means confined exclusively to Americans) of small-town Americana, a nostalgia for a 'suburban pastoral' of football pennants, chocolate malteds and high-school proms, a nostalgia all the more potent and seductive for embodying a craving for something that never existed, not even when the films that indulged it were made. (In these recessionary, war-shadowed nineties, that no doubt accounts for a great deal of their current appeal.) And there was above all the fact that, although originally filmed and released over a period of nine years (from 1937 to 1946), they were screened by Channel 4 at regular weekly intervals. The principal effect of such a radical compression of time was, in a quite brutal manner, to telescope the ageing process as it affected Mickey Rooney himself, who was 17 when the series started and 26 when it was complete. And the brutality was further underscored by our own hindsight knowledge that, at least in the physical sense, Rooney never really did 'grow up', our knowledge that the grinning, fresh-faced, bushy-tailed adolescent of the *Andy Hardy* films would eventually be transformed into the paunchy leprechaun who could be seen in the burlesque musical *Sugar Babies* three or four years ago at the Savoy Theatre. (Indeed, this whole question of ageing on film is a fascinating one, and it would be instructive to juxtapose movie stills of young actors playing old men – the name of Orson Welles springs most immediately to mind – with photographs of the old men they themselves were to become 'in life'.)

As for the Barbican retrospective, although it perhaps predictably concentrates on films of recent date, it does contain most of the titles one might have expected, *My Life as a Dog, Au revoir les enfants, Salaam Bombay, Cinema Paradiso,* and a few one might not have expected, the Japanese *Muddy River*, the Israeli *Summer of Aviva* and the Chinese *Summer at Grandpa's* – with, hearteningly, not a single Hollywood production in sight. (Also being screened is one of the greatest of all films about childhood, that magnificent Bergmanesque bergamasque, *Fanny and Alexander*.)

I regret, however, one (unavoidable) omission, of a marvellous film which, as far as I know, has never been accorded a commercial presentation anywhere, Raul Ruiz's rich and strange version of

Treasure Island with a cosmopolitan cast that includes Jean-Pierre Léaud, Martin Landau, the French pop singer Sheila and, as Long John Silver, the American actor Vic Tayback (late of the television sitcom *Alice*). I regret its absence not only because it's the finest, if equally the most bizarre, of the medium's umpteen adaptations of Stevenson's novel but also because it bears out in vivid fashion my comments above about the poignancy of ageing in the cinema.

Before attending a private screening some years ago, I chanced to ask Ruiz about his Jim Hawkins, Melvil Poupaud, an exquisitely sultry little boy whom he had already cast in several of his films. 'Oh,' he replied, in his typically expansive style, 'Melvil became an adolescent during the shoot. It's visible in the film. But be careful not to blink – it happens from one shot to the next!'

Raul's friends soon grow accustomed to such baroquely Ruizian hyperbole – yet there it was, precisely as he claimed, up there on the screen. A close-up portrait shot of Melvil, still a pre-pubescent child. A reaction shot of Sheila. Then the camera returns to Melvil, who is now visibly a pubescent youth. According to Raul, these three shots were filmed in sequence on the same day.

The art of luxury

An amusing 'literal' contrived to squeak into one of the musical programmes of last year's Edinburgh Festival: *Le Sucre du Printemps*. From *Le Sacre* to *Le Sucre*, from the ritualistic to the sugary – it was ever thus, perhaps, with aesthetic modernism, and Stravinsky's fiery, ground-breaking piece, regarded as it now is as a not too taxing, not too rebarbative item in any orchestral concert, offers a striking case in point.

It should not be forgotten, however, that, no matter how celebrated the furore surrounding its première, the *Sacre* was commissioned by Diaghilev for his Ballets Russes, a company whose seasons are still recalled by a waning band of elderly balletomanes as spectacles of an unparalleled – and for the most part unproblematic – gorgeousness. From 1909 to Diaghilev's death in Venice twenty years later, the original Ballets Russes did indeed represent a radical and progressive force in the culture of the twentieth century, but it was founded on an aesthetic whose dominant ideology was one of patronage, élitism and above all *luxury*. And I have sometimes wondered whether the decline and ultimate demise of that aesthetic – basically a prettified corruption of the Wagnerian *Gesamtkunstwerk*, in which the finest composers would be engaged to provide scores (Stravinsky, Debussy, Ravel, etc.), the finest painters to create décors (Picasso, Derain, Gris), the finest couturiers to design costumes (most notably, Chanel) and even the finest writers to devise scenarios or, as they call them in the ballet world, with no doubt good reason, 'arguments' (Cocteau, Claudel, Hofmannsthal) – have derived less from economic considerations or egalitarian convictions than from a Puritanical and now prevalent belief that luxury is anathema to serious art.

What brought this to mind was the Covent Garden production of Richard Strauss's *Capriccio* with costumes by the Italian couturier Gianni Versace, a concurrent exhibition of Versace's theatrical work at the Royal College of Art (so dazzling that one returns from it *bronzed*) and the revival of Jean Anouilh's *The Rehearsal* at the Garrick, costumed by Jasper Conran – all of them, potentially, experiences of a certain artistic luxury.

Versace's designs received a generally hostile press. Max Loppert in the *Financial Times* found the show 'gruesomely overdressed' and Richard Morrison in *The Times* complained that the stage had been turned into a catwalk. What *are* they talking about? Apart from some agreeably loud Terry-Thomasish waistcoats for the males, and scarlet livery for the servants, the spectator's eye is drawn, as it properly should be, to Kiri Te Kanawa, who wears a beautiful long-sleeved afternoon coat for most of the performance before switching to a brilliantly beaded evening gown for her final solo. Strauss's opera, a witty, 'civilised', unashamedly élitist disquisition on the whole nature of musical drama, is set among the elegant, leisured upper classes and could not plausibly be staged in any less moneyed milieu. And the costumes, in both cut and cloth, are the real McCoy, unlike the horrid Conran gowns in *The Rehearsal*, which attempt in vain to marry *haute couture* forms to low-quality fabrics. So why such a terror of glamour?

The primary reason is probably of a sociomoral nature: How can one defend a spectacle whose motto might be 'Give us this day our daily cake' when so many in the world – some of them, as it happens, perfectly visible in their cardboard boxes from the entrance of the Royal Opera House – are being denied their daily bread? Yet opera in general and Strauss's opera in particular, not to mention the prohibitively pricey Covent Garden itself, are all, in their various ways, *objets de luxe*, and hence, if one cared to make something out of it, quite as objectionable as any contained display of luxury on stage. The second reason is rooted in a question of taste, or rather distaste, that peculiarly British distaste for the figure of Harlequin, judged vulgar because he wears his coat inside-out, as if colour were only for linings. And the third reason, encompassing both of the others, can be related to a general cultural zeitgeist, one that frowns upon almost every manifestation of gaiety and charm.

But one wonders whether and why, even in such troubled times, it need be so. During the interwar years, after all, a period that was hardly starved of political crises, there were, alongside the adherents of the dodecaphonic school, a number of composers still happily producing light, divertimento-type scores with titles like *Parade*, *Façade* and *Salade*, whereas most new compositions one hears of these days are burdened with names more redolent of scientific than of artistic experimentation – *Plus Minus One* and *Frames, Pulse and Interruptions* and *Polyphonie X* and *H P S C H D* and *Time and Motion Study*. In the twenties, too, painters like Picasso and Miró, Braque and Léger (with his wonderful liquorice allsort figures), would take an occasional day off from revolutionising their chosen medium to design an eye-fetching poster or drop-curtain, whereas only Hockney appears now to possess that sort of 'occasional' talent and be prepared to exercise it.

And yet, I repeat, why so? It may seem a frivolous question, and I certainly wouldn't suggest that modern composers and painters devote themselves exclusively to cheering us up, but surely contributing to the gaiety of nations, as they say, is a high and noble pursuit for any artist?

The bombs are dropping around me (on television) as I write this, the Scuds are flying, the Gulf is in flames. Wherever my thoughts may wander, however, I am still a professional writer on the arts: in the words of another Stravinsky piece, *L'Histoire du soldat*, composed in the not exactly uneventful year of 1917, 'Je fais mon métier, monsieur, mon petit métier.' Art, too, is not only a calling or a vocation. It's also a job, a métier – that of making beautiful things for an ugly world.

War movies and movie wars

American sociopsychologists have already coined a term for it: CNN Complex, or an addiction to news bulletins fuelled by the pathological fear of missing something of significance. It is a condition to which I fell victim on the second night of the Gulf war, which was also the night of the first missile raid on Israel, when CNN's journalists struggled manfully to continue reporting through their gas masks and the station's New York anchorman, Tom Brokaw, visibly blanched (as I myself did) at the notion that the attack might have been chemical in origin.

That piece of confused (and, as we learned the following morning, misinformed) reportage, a reportage which operated on the viewer without anaesthetic, strikes me as a genuine and possibly irreversible turning point in our relationship with the media. For what CNN communicated to those of us who were watching it live was not so much 'news' of an event as 'the event itself' before it had been turned into news. (In past wars, the news was invariably subsequent to – and, if it was grim enough, on occasion deliberately misleading about – the event it was supposed to be reporting on.) And even if, as predigested information, the news remains crucial to our capacity to contextualise an event, I cannot help thinking it no bad thing that we British and American viewers, thousands of miles away from the theatre of war, should also from time to time be made privy to the event itself, to its mounting panic, its dread-inducing harums and scarums, its false and its true alarms. If, like the Israelis themselves, we tossed and turned all night with anxiety, so much the better.

The incident also underscored the heightening visibility of another conspicuous sociocultural relationship – that which exists between recent television coverage of the Gulf war and the whole genre of the American war movie.

It's easy enough cataloguing a few of the more superficial levels on which their two iconographies have begun to feast off one another.

On the one hand, there is the fact that a film entitled *Hangfire* is already on release in the United States. It's a low-budget 'action-adventurer', as *Variety* would put it, its plot centring on a trio of escaped convicts who take a small American town hostage, and there would be nothing to distinguish this particular specimen from any other of the genre were it not that its advertising slogan is 'Saddam Hussein Look Out!' The film is set entirely within the American hinterland and makes no direct allusion to the Gulf war. Yet, for its producer, one Steve Stabler, 'the analogy to current events is pretty obvious'. Is it? And who exactly is it that Saddam should be looking out for? The three jailbirds? The besieged townfolk? Or perhaps Hollywood producers like Stabler? For even before the end of the conflict the film industry's mythmakers are already at work, and *Hangfire* is only one of several new American films hoping to catch the Gulf war on the wing.

On the other hand, one might mention the *Top Gun* enthusiasm of many of the youthful American pilots for their hi-tech bombers; a US army disc-jockey's 'Goooooooood Morning, Saudi Arabia!'; the universally remarked-upon resemblance of General Schwarzkopf's demonstration of precision bombing to a video game (although no one thought to point out that, since video games are designed precisely to simulate aerial combat conditions, it would be odd if such a resemblance didn't exist); the virtual absence, or *abeyance*, of the enemy, as in numerous Vietnam movies; and so forth.

There exist, however, at least three slightly more subtle ways in which our responses to the media's war have been influenced, even conditioned, by the cinema.

First, like CNN's coverage in the Gulf, war movies are far better at describing than analysing. Thus Oliver Stone's film *Platoon* was widely criticised for failing to address the causes of American involvement in South-East Asia but just as widely praised for the vividness with which it conveyed the Vietnam experience, the unsettling sense, as I phrased it in my book *Hollywood's Vietnam*, that every American soldier 'who happens to find himself within the camera's field of vision is *already* in danger'. That sense is conveyed equally vividly by current TV reporting. As one watches these plucky journalists in the thick of things, one cannot still a nagging apprehension that they are going to be blown to bits even as they speak; as one listens to John Simpson reporting from Baghdad by satellite telephone and then being abruptly cut off, one cannot help half-suspecting that he has just been skewered by an Iraqi bayonet. This, for war correspondents, is the year of living dangerously.

Second, the loving display of precision weaponry, of those glossy 'smart' bombs that, like filter-tipped cigarettes, are designed to weed out the nicotine of indiscriminate destruction, recalls a masterpiece of a film, Stanley Kubrick's *Dr Strangelove*, that said absolutely everything there is to be said about the chronic bellicosity of American foreign policy. What *Strangelove* captured as no film had done before or has done since is the seductive sexuality, the rampant phallicism, of modern warfare, a phallicism evident in the now famous video footage of a missile penetrating an air shaft and producing the kind of orgasm that, as they say, 'makes the ceiling move'.

Finally, there is the way in which, in the popular imagination, Saddam Hussein himself has become a concentration of pure malevolence, of a type instantly, irresistibly, reminiscent of the flamboyant villains in James Bond movies. For what we have here, as in each of the episodes in the Bond cycle, is an 'evil genius' holding the world to ransom, threatening it with the kind of weaponry that 'should only be in the hands of the superpowers', setting the Kuwaiti oilfields alight, and so on. The snag, alas, is that we would seem to have no 007 on our side for Saddam to confront in some bunker in Baghdad, sneering 'So, Mr Bond, we meet at last!' before being put out of commission once and for all.

In fact, when I come to think of it, the sole image common to both wars and war movies which hasn't yet (as I write) been beamed across the world is that, curiously, of a victim, a single dead person.

The wind in the trees

The National Film Theatre recently premièred the latest film by a director (or, rather, two directors) widely, if often grudgingly, recognised as being among the most important in the world. Scant publicity attended the event, and to my knowledge I am the only journalist even to allude to its having taken place. The film was *Cézanne*, a fifty-minute meditation on the painter and his work by Jean-Marie Straub and his wife Danièle Huillet (who are still probably best-known for their *Chronik der Anna Magdalena Bach* of 1968); and if I see anything finer this year, as reviewers say, I shall be very much surprised.

But then, just about the finest film I saw last year was *Der Tod des Empedokles (The Death of Empedocles)*, the Straubs' adaptation of an incomplete verse drama by Hölderlin, another version of which they subsequently filmed as *Schwarze Sunde (Black Sin)*. Both were screened one evening at the Goethe Institute in South Kensington and the only journalistic attention that that performance received was an excellent short article by Julian Petley in *Sight and Sound*. Petley quoted Straub himself, who introduced the screening, as saying: 'It's really scandalous that when a film like this is shown for the first time in Britain there's nothing about it in the press.'

That may be immodest; it also happens to be indisputable. With the arts media in this country now all but hypnotised by a degenerate American cinema, a cinema of inflation and escalation (whose shrill, egregious archetype would be David Lynch's *Wild At Heart*), the Straubs offer a counter-example of unbullying serenity and calm. Straub and Huillet are, in fact, among the very few contemporary (non-Third World) filmmakers who, in a medium monopolised by the city and the automobile, know how to film the countryside – something of a lost art since the end of the silent period, the deaths of Renoir and Pagnol and the decline of the western. And I recall a prescient remark made by D. W. Griffith fully sixty years ago, one which Straub himself has frequently endorsed: 'What modern movies lack is the wind in the trees.' There exists, to be sure, a significant theoretical dimension to the Straubs' work, which is no doubt what causes most ordinary audiences to recoil from it in terror. But what, by contrast, renders their films such *magical* experiences, at least for a properly motivated spectator, is precisely this capacity, one they share with the great silent masters, with Renoir and Pagnol, with Howard Hawks,

John Ford and Anthony Mann, to film the wind in the trees, to film vibration, to film *air*.

As for the Hollywood mainstream product, I have to say that it's with ever diminishing enthusiasm that I go to any American film these days, and whenever I begin to feel that I am being bullied (as, lately, by Coppola's new *Godfather*, a monstrosity), I simply get up and walk out. Every so often, though, a film does manage to squeak through the system which impresses me as having assimilated in its fashion the Straubian value of restraint, of a certain emotional austerity. (Not, of course, that there has been the slightest question of influence.)

Reversal of Fortune, for example. What is so unorthodox about Barbet Schroeder's cool, stylish, Mankiewicz-line fictionalisation of the Claus von Bülow case is the manner in which it teases both the genre to which it belongs and the mainstream audience at which it is aimed. For here, after all, is a courtroom drama which does not boast a single extended scene in a courtroom, a murder plot which is narrated by the victim (who herself is in a coma as she narrates it), and a villain the nature of whose villainy, left unproven, has actually (and, when you think of it, outrageously) ceased to matter very much by the end of the film.

The Grifters, for its part, is based on one of those so-called dime novels of which cinematic adaptations are now a dime a dozen – it's not only Anjelica Huston's presence that makes one think of the film as 'Hustonian'. Yet, if it's rather more interesting than most such recent *film noir* pastiches, it's because of its near-total repudiation of pulp atmospherics (which is to say, the kind of 'cheap' poetry that cost fifty million dollars to recreate in *Dick Tracy*); because most of the crimes committed in the film unexpectedly turn out to be *crimes passionnels*; and, above all, because Stephen Frears's direction is so cold, neutral and distanced from the action that, when violence does erupt, it takes one, as it should, totally by surprise (unlike that in *GoodFellas*, let's say, which is strictly generic, a Scorsese trademark).

As for *Mr and Mrs Bridge*, its refusal to toe the Hollywood party line is exemplified by the much-criticised climactic twist in which Mrs Bridge, locked inside a snowbound automobile, does not after all die of hypothermia: for, whereas a narrative 'twist' in the cinema usually means something happening that you didn't expect to happen, in James Ivory's film it means something not happening that you did expect to happen. In reality, nothing much ever does happen in this film, but it is at times, for all that, intensely moving. The reason for that is Ivory's treatment of love. Although, on the surface, the Bridges' life together is as emotionally anaesthetised as the film itself appears to be in its deliberately buttoned-up style, there *are* brief instants when love (Mrs Bridge's timorous love for her stiff stuffed-shirt of a husband and, even more movingly, Mr Bridge's almost totally unarticulated love for her) is granted expression. And the point is that the impact of these epiphanies would have been far less powerful had the film not rejected the bullying, hysterical tone to which, in another director's hands, the same material might well have lent itself.

It's easy enough to film the external signs of love, but Ivory's achievement is to have filmed the intangibility of Love itself, to have allowed it to circulate through his film, as invisible yet as indispensable as . . . well, as air.

The poetry of embarrassment

It was while watching on television, for what was probably the third or fourth time, George Stevens's magnificent 1935 film adaptation of the Booth Tarkington novel *Alice Adams* that I was re-alerted to the terrible *poetry* of embarrassment. Alice, played by Katharine Hepburn, is an intelligent, 'artistic' young woman whose sole offence is to be ashamed of her lower-middle-class family. Invited to a country-club ball given by a socialite acquaintance, and wearing a faded party dress from the year before last ('Organdy?' bitches one guest to her equally incredulous companion: 'Perhaps *we're* wrong'), poor Alice struggles all evening to convey the impression that it's out of choice and not circumstance that she isn't dancing. With the glassily dazed smile of the lonely and unloved, she gamely hails total strangers as old acquaintances, girlishly flutters her bedraggled nosegay and, when tactfully asked after, feigns exhaustion as though from a surfeit of foxtrots. The situation in itself is painful enough; and because of the subtle, on occasion practically imperceptible, modulations of terror in Hepburn's performance, what one ends by wishing for both Alice and oneself is for the earth to open up and engulf her.

It was many years ago that I saw *Alice Adams* for the first time, but nothing I have been exposed to since has dimmed the horror of that scene, not even such subsequent (and unintended, quite unpoetic embarrassments as the nightmarish first night of the RSC revival of *The Happiest Days Of Your Life*, when one of the cast members failed to recall a single line of dialogue throughout the entire performance, or Bryan Forbes's now infamous production of *Macbeth*, when Peter O'Toole emerged from the murder of Banquo so outlandishly bloodstained as to resemble a gargantuan bottle of tomato ketchup, or Julian Clary's show the other evening at the Aldwych when – but no, that particular experience was so very, so exquisitely, embarrassing I cannot bring myself to evoke it in print.

Significantly, the adjective 'exqusite' is often used to describe situations of both embarrassment and pain, which suggests that some of us at least might actually be drawn to these spectacles out of a latent sadomasochistic *craving* for mortification, as though it were as pleasurable to feel embarrassed in the theatre or cinema as it is to feel petrified on a funfair ride. That, certainly, is the thesis of Francis Wyndham's essay, 'The Theatre of Embarrassment', which gives its title to a recently published collection of his journalism. Wyndham's assertion is that the theatre as an art form is consciously founded on the seduction of embarrassment, that while 'the spectators imagine that they are hoping to witness some actor give the greatest performance of his life, never to be repeated in exactly the same way, they are also wondering if he may not give the *worst*'. He continues: 'The people in the audience have paid money in the hope that they will be made to feel some emotion – pity, terror, mirth, lust, interest, sympathy, outrage. In circumstances as conducive as these to intense embarrassment, they very naturally feel embarrassed; relieved at feeling *something*, and therefore getting their money's worth, they mistake the shock of embarrassment for whatever emotion the play is intended to inspire.'

Although such an idea had never occurred to me before, it strikes me now as incontrovertible. And it seems to me that Wyndham's sole error of judgment (in another article in the same collection on Marlene Dietrich's cabaret appearances in the sixties) is in attributing to every audience 'a streak of masochism'. I would propose, instead, that the masochism is almost completely on the performer's part and that the audience is more properly to be described as sadistic. (In a sadomasochistic relationship, to be sure, it's not always a simple matter distinguishing the sadistic from the masochistic.) An audience, after all, is an only slightly more refined version of a mob baying for blood.

If that analogy applies to every kind of audience, however, it is most acutely relevant to showbiz and opera fanatics. These are people, I am convinced, who actually *prefer* the Dietrich of her declining years to that of her heyday, who *want* her masklike features to look stiff and waxen. Similarly, they *wanted* the ageing, drugged and overweight Judy Garland to trip over both her microphone wire and her lines. They *wanted* Maria Callas's voice to croak on high Cs that it once attained with triumphant impunity. And, in the rather more modest context of the current show at the Aldwych, they *want* Julian Clary's hapless 'guests' to be hauled up on to the stage and subjected to indignities that will haunt them for many a night thereafter. There is a very fine line indeed between what Wyndham calls 'the fascinating fear of failure' and a morbid desire for it.

Granted, this compulsion to demean stars (women in particular, one cannot help noticing) is a half-conscious, perhaps even completely unconscious, condition, and most audiences would indignantly reject such a theory. Yet, watching Julian Clary put his victims through their degrading hoops, I was reminded again of Andy Warhol's dictum on fifteen-minute celebrity and found myself wondering whether the peculiar appeal of Clary's show derives precisely from the manner in which it condenses the whole career-long parabola of fame, from initial gratification to ultimate humiliation, into a single (and *mauvais*) *quart d'heure*.

The TV and the teeshirt

'I would never think to switch one on but if I do happen to catch one, I'm immediately hooked.' That observation, concerning wildlife programmes on television, is one I tend to hear with quite extraordinary frequency. It's an observation, indeed, I fairly frequently make myself, except that, in my own case, what I'm especially partial to is undersea footage. And, having long pondered the peculiar fascination of such footage, I've come to the conclusion that, apart from the inherent interest of the filmed material, its appeal to me resides above all in the fact that I, as a viewer, appear to be seeing exactly what the diver-cum-cameraman sees, that what swims (literally) across his field of vision swims (figuratively) across mine, almost as though the television set had become a sort of bathysphere, its screen offering me a mirror image, as it were, of the oblong 'screen' of the diver's own mask.

There is nothing 'live' about such material, of course, but it may well be the next best thing. For with so little live television around these days, it has been rendered increasingly difficult to calculate the number of layers of representation any programme must traverse before 'what happened' is finally communicated to the viewer.

Consider again that celebrated video footage from the Gulf war of one of the American army's 'smart' bombs penetrating the air shaft of its target before detonating – footage which seemed to bring the reality of the conflict into the viewer's own living-room with unparalleled candour and immediacy. Yet the bomber first had to select his target, the video cameraman his angle, the Pentagon which one out of presumably hundreds of such videos to screen to journalists during its briefing session and the television companies how much of that video to show the viewer (who in his own turn retains the right, by selecting one channel over another, to decide whether or not to watch it).

Or, from a totally different context, think of the distance that has to be covered by a film from its original manifestation as a pristine new print released by some studio in the sixties, say, to what is left of it when it turns up on television in the nineties, with its widescreen format scanned-and-panned, its colour fading, the rhythm of its narrative pulverised by commercial breaks, its dialogue possibly censored and the degree of information contained in each and every one of its images virtually halved by the far poorer definition of the TV screen. (Honey, I shrunk the cinema!)

In spite of this shrinkage, however, it would be foolish to dismiss television, as some have done, as a mere wastebasket of second-hand sounds and images. Rather, it is one of the twin *terminals* of all basic circuits of information. And the other? That is, I suggest . . . the teeshirt.

The very first message-bearing teeshirts I remember noticing in this country (except for the odd one blazoning the logo of a generally pretty obscure American college) had imprinted on the front a grim portrait of Beethoven. Other composers followed – Mozart, Brahms, I even recollect a lone Sibelius. At which point the floodgates were opened, and it soon reached the stage where the teeshirt had been recognised as a whole new communicating surface, free to bear any message, any image, the wearer pleased – portraits of film, rock and sports stars, lewd cartoons, advertisements, personalised publicity, souvenirs of pop concerts and street sit-ins, political slogans, newspaper headlines ('Gotcha!'), song lyrics ('I Can't Get No Satisfaction'), even self-referential jokes ('My parents visited London and all they brought me back was this lousy teeshirt').

But perhaps I am alone in actually *reading* other people's teeshirts, which I do as idly but as nosily as I sometimes find myself glancing at a flickering TV screen through an uncurtained ground-floor window. Certainly, the wearers themselves rapidly cease to be conscious of the particular message which they carry through the streets like so many sandwich men and women: it becomes so much part of the composite image they present to the world that they must eventually lose all sense of its informational value. And one cannot help wondering whether the ultimate avatar of every form of information or representation is to be *worn*. Thus the woman who wears a Gianni Versace gown one of whose decorative motifs is the codified Warhol image of Marilyn Monroe (an image, it's worth noting, that, before it became just one component of an elaborate design, was a silk-screen replication of a photograph of an actress who herself, before being reinvented by Hollywood, had been a troubled young woman named Norma Jean Baker) cannot be expected to remain sensitive for long to the fact that such an image once had a real meaning.

The TV and the teeshirt – I wouldn't care to extend the analogy too far between a signifying system as sophisticated as the former and one as primitive as the latter. But it occurs to me nevertheless that television also risks becoming too much part of ourselves, of our quotidian round; that it risks becoming something we 'wear' without any longer realising that we are wearing it. Granted, most of us are perfectly capable of processing the messages it sends out to us, but our response to these messages still tends to be, at the very deepest level, both uncritical and incommunicable. In an age when practically every channel of communication is vulnerable to the misreadings and outright falsifications of mechanical reproduction, relatively few of us take the trouble to assess the extent to which sounds and images have been mediated before reaching us. We are not yet, in short, what might be called tele-literate.

And should you still be unconvinced of the possibility of ingesting information without consciously conceptualising it, here is a little test. If you see someone in the street looking at his watch, instantly approach him and ask him the time. On nine occasions out of ten he will be obliged to consult his watch all over again to give you the information you need.

What do men want?

'What do women want?' Since women are important *to* (if considerably less so *in*) a still predominantly male American cinema, pragmatic paraphrases of the immemorial Freudian poser continue to exercise the collective Hollywood 'intelligence': 'What (type of films) do women (spectators) want?' or 'What (type of men) do women (characters) want?' or 'What (type of roles) do women (performers) want?'

From the evidence of those actresses (Meryl Streep, Julia Roberts, Michelle Pfeiffer, etc.) who are currently mistresses of their own professional destinies, the anwer to the last question would appear to be the sort of strong, feisty, liberated roles that their most illustrious elders, the Crawfords and Stanwycks and Hepburns, had to fight to secure. And, as Barry Norman would say, why not? The problem, though, is that appearances can be deceptive and that, even if 'meaty' feminine roles are in the ascendant these days, women in Hollywood movies seem obstinately fated to remain passive objects – rather than becoming genuinely active subjects – of desire. In fact, it even happens on occasion that when a film can claim a strong 'feminine' subject it's an actor, not an actress, who is chosen to personify it. In *Kramer vs Kramer*, for example, it was almost as though Dustin Hoffman were determined to demonstrate that men made better mothers than women; and in *Tootsie* that men made better women than women!

These were extreme cases, but consider a trio of films (two of them relatively recent, the other brand new), each of which enshrines the kind of big, splashy role any actress would supposedly crave to get her teeth into.

In *Fatal Attraction* Glenn Close played a high-flying career woman who, spurned by her married lover (Michael Douglas), wreaks demented revenge on both him and his family. What, you might ask, could be less passive than that? Yet, no matter that it gave her an opportunity to chew up the scenery, the casting was nothing short of an insult to Close. As conceived, after all, the character had to be both sexy (otherwise, why would Douglas have put his marriage at risk?) and crazy (otherwise, how could one credit her subsequent unhingement?). So the makers of the film cast Close, presumably on the offensive grounds that she was capable of looking both sexy and crazy at once; they saddled her character with a frizzy, corkscrewy hairdo suggestive equally of a cover girl (sexy) and a bag lady (crazy); they installed her in a glitzily appointed apartment (sexy) but located that apartment in an area of Manhattan as insalubrious as a suburb of Hell (crazy); and so on. The word for this is of course manipulation, of the actress as much as the audience.

Or take Jodie Foster, awarded an Oscar, Hollywood's gilded dildo, for her performance as a victim of gang-rape in *The Accused*, a film widely admired as 'feminist'. (Foster's lawyer in the narrative was also a woman, the cool, saintly Kelly McGillis.) The long rape sequence itself, in a sleazy small-town barroom, was symptomatic of what was so hopelessly wrong with the central character. Surrounded by leering rednecks, Foster leans lasciviously over a jukebox, a cigarette dangling sluttishly from her lips, as though it were about to be jerked away by a whiplash. She is drugged to the eyeballs, her face is bleary and smeary with make-up, her breasts are practically popping out of her shirt, her skirt is crotch-high. (This is a fair, unbiased, unslavering description of what is up there, visible to all, on the screen.) And then she starts to wiggle her hips. In fact, she wiggles her hips so salaciously I couldn't help feeling that the director (Jonathan Kaplan, for the record) hoped to provoke the audience beyond endurance, to provoke even liberals, *even women*, to such a fever of suspense that, no matter our abhorrence of rape, and primarily to relieve the tension, we would all start to cry out in unison, 'For God's sake get it over with! Rape her!' Whereupon the film, drawing itself up to its full height, would wag a self-righteous finger at us as though to say, 'No! Not even *this* pathetic excuse for womanhood deserves to be raped!'

It may be good polemics (although I doubt it, especially with a rape so graphically filmed), but it seems to me above all to degrade the actress by obliging her to incarnate yet another male-inspired stereotype of femininity – in this instance, the tabloid cliché of 'the sort of woman who asks for it'. And the role itself serves merely to illustrate the thesis, being utterly devoid of autonomous character and life.

The most recent, most subtle and in some ways most disturbing example of such exploitation is Mia Farrow's performance in Woody Allen's new film, *Alice*. Now, whatever one's opinion of Allen's work, one has always tended to think of it as progressive, generous and, where Farrow is concerned, actually very magnanimous. Indeed, to the chagrin of some of his admirers, Allen has gradually been effacing himself as a performer in favour of his wife and Muse, and many of his later films (*The Purple Rose of Cairo, September, Another Woman*) have been structured around her. This is also true of *Alice*, whose theme is a woman's midlife crisis of identity and whose model (with Woody Allen there is always a model) is patently Fellini's *Juliet of the Spirits*. Through the ministrations of a mysterious Chinese herbalist timorous little Alice contrives to communicate with a deceased old flame, transform herself into a brazen seductress, render herself invisible and find ultimate, improbable fulfilment as the Mother Teresa of the Lower East Side.

The film is very minor Woody, a slight, bitter-sweet, tolerably watchable comedy. But, as one does watch it, an uneasy suspicion grows – the suspicion that the herbalist is serving exactly the same function as the ghostly Bogart in *Play It Again, Sam* and, most uncannily, that *Mia Farrow has turned into Woody Allen*. If one closes one's eyes, her whiny, schlemiel-like delivery begins to sound identical to his, her voice seems only an octave or two highter; if one half-closes one's eyes, her face, beautiful as it still is, could almost be mistaken for her husband's.

From Zelig, the human chameleon, to Svengali, the human vampire-bat – that of late has been the trajectory of Allen's career. And that, perhaps, in Hollywood, is what men want.

The way we live now

In *La Chambre claire* (or, in English, *Camera Lucida*), his book-length essay on photography, Barthes used the Latin term *punctum* to designate any ostensibly minor, unbelaboured detail in the photographic image which nevertheless, and often contrary to the photographer's own intention, draws the eye inexorably towards it. On the reasonable assumption, then, that the term should be equally applicable to the written word, what is the *punctum* in this sentence (extracted from a *Radio Times* 'blurb' for the children's film *The Love Bug*): 'The Disney classic in which Herbie, the gallant

Volkswagen beetle with a mind of his own, comes to the rescue of a young racing driver and the girl he loves'?

The answer is 'classic'. Or, rather, that would be the answer were 'classic' not now a word whose meaning has been irrevocably debased by persistent misuse and indiscriminate repetition. The other week, in the same magazine, the film *Dentist in the Chair* was also judged a 'classic' (with Bob Monkhouse and Kenneth Connor, for heaven's sake!). In a recent *Sunday Times* the critic Dilys Powell cited John Huston's *The Bible*, by wellnigh universal consent one of the director's feeblest films, as having been 'described as a classic', which it certainly never was until now. TV shows like *Dad's Army* and *Up Pompeii* are routinely accorded 'classic' status. A Maxwell House commercial complacently promotes its 'classic' brand of coffee. And the Virago publishing house has catalogued its entire range of reissues from, mostly, the interwar years under 'Modern Classics'.

Although in none of these instances can the word be said to have assumed its proper meaning (the relevant definition in the OED is 'of the first class, of the highest rank or importance; approved as a model'), in each of them it can be interpreted easily enough. Thus, in the case of 'classic' films on television, it probably means 'repeated so often they have become as familiar as classics'. With revived situation comedies it means merely 'better than what's on now'. Where Maxwell House is concerned, the idea was doubtless to distinguish the original mix from various newfangled blends which haven't quite caught on. As for Virago's Modern Classics, there the ambition is surely a polemical one, the very moot implication being that a number of contemporary literary masterpieces have been undervalued solely because their authors were women.

These novels may in effect have been undervalued, but promoting each and every one of them as a 'classic' is in turn to devalue the word – to the point where one becomes chary of any new work of art so described, especially if it should be qualified by the Maxwell Houseish tag 'instant'. 'Instant classic', however, is precisely the description that preceded the arrival in this country of Susan Sontag's short fiction *The Way We Live Now*, which first appeared in a single issue of the *New Yorker* and has just been published here in book form by Jonathan Cape with a handful of (in truth, rather redundant) 'abstract illustrations' by the British painter Howard Hodgkin. The subject of Sontag's story is Aids (she has already written a disappointing study of *Aids and Its Metaphors*), and royalties from the Cape edition will be forwarded to appropriate charities both here and in the United States.

I don't know if *The Way We Live Now* is an 'instant classic' – I am not even sure I know what such a near-oxymoron would look or sound like – but I do know that its central conceit is a stroke of genius on Sontag's part. The fact that neither the dying protagonist nor the disease from which he is dying is named, the fact that he is bizarrely *absent* from the narrative, his existence defined exclusively by those who come to visit him, may at first impinge on the reader as a purely literary strategy, a self-consciously fastidious avoidance of the morbid and the overly obvious. (Just as the fact that there are as many women as men at his bedside, some of which women are former lovers of his, may seem a too explicit concern on Sontag's part not to be seen reducing the disease to its homosexual factor and thereby reinforcing a still common prejudicial myth about its incidence.) In reality, though, this spectral non-presence reflects a profound truth about every condition close to death: that it constitutes a solitude which the friend, the intimate, the bedside well-wisher can approach but never penetrate; that one can only ever be a *midwife of death*, as attentive to, but also as detached from, the experience as a midwife is to and from that of giving birth; and that, ultimately, the only truly serious illnesses are those which are suffered by oneself, any illness suffered by another, even an intimate friend, being always (let's admit it) just that crucial little bit less serious.

Within the hushed babel of voices hovering round the deathbed Sontag contrives unerringly to hone in on the nervous community of commiseration, the sometimes unseemly jockeying for position and rank, the inevitable factionalising of close and distant friends (as one refers to close and distant relations). If, throughout, she tends to remain on the surface of things (the story is by a very long way the least dissectional, least analytical of her writings, fact or fiction), it's all the more effectively to tease their exposed nerve ends. And she rejects, rightly, I believe, the pathos and melodrama of the countdown and leaves her protagonist alive, just, at the end.

But now let's return to that word 'classic', which is, as I tried to show, at risk of becoming what ethnologists term a *mana*, defined by Lévi-Strauss as 'an indeterminate value of signification, devoid of meaning in itself and capable of receiving any meaning whatsoever.' (An obvious example is 'fuck'.) If *The Way We Live Now* is indeed a classic, it is because, in a literary context, it finally accords Aids what the French would call its *titres de noblesse*, its 'claims to nobility'. And, perhaps, at the same time – albeit, I suspect, all too fleetingly – it will give back its *titres de noblesse* to the word 'classic' itself.

Come back to the NFT, Jimmy Dean, Jimmy Dean

I was once permitted to view the screen tests that François Truffaut shot in 1958 for his very first film, *Les 400 Coups*. All of them were naturally of interest, but the footage I was most anxious to see was of Jean-Pierre Léaud, the non-professional who would eventually land the part of fourteen-year-old Antoine Doinel and become an emblematic icon of the New Wave. The test did not require Léaud to act; he simply had to respond to a few deliberately trite queries (concerning his hobbies, his schoolwork, what motivated him to audition, etc.) put to him offscreen by the director. Even from such partial evidence, however, it was rapidly made plain to the viewer that *Truffaut invented nothing*. What we tend to think of as Doinel's 'character' in the sequence of five films that Truffaut made about him was already indelibly present in Léaud's 'personality' – so that, for the test, he had merely to *act out* what he already *was*, glazing his kittenish, Keatonish little face (albeit of an animated, smiling Keaton) into a snug, malleable mask of itself.

It's quite a curious business being made retrospectively privy to what might be called the prehistory of an actor's career. Is the talent already visible, one wonders, even if still more or less untapped? Would one have been capable of spotting that talent in a film that was never intended to be a 'vehicle' for it? And is it not as difficult, when judging so primitive a performance, to ignore the omniscience of hindsight as it must be for a jury to disregard some damning if improperly submitted piece of evidence? It is questions like these which are raised by the National Film Theatre's current retrospective of the early television work of James Dean.

Before being selected by Elia Kazan to play the leading role in *East of Eden* in 1955, it turns out that Dean worked fairly extensively in television, for most of the time specialising in the same type of character, the broody, eternally alienated adolescent, with which he would later be associated in the cinema. (There is at least one bizarre exception in the NFT season, though, *The Thief*, an adaptation of *Le Voleur*, a typically 'well-made' melodrama by Henry Bernstein which has him, as the coddled if misunderstood son of an aristocratic French family at the turn of the century, rather maladroitly endeavouring to combine the boyish with the Charles Boyerish.) And, as with Truffaut and Léaud, it is very soon clear that, on a certain level, neither Kazan nor Nicholas Ray (who was to direct him in *Rebel Without a Cause*) nor George Stevens (who was to direct him in *Giant*) invented anything. Everything Dean subsequently became he already was. The mytho-iconography of his mannerisms had gelled and was already even slightly self-parodic: the shy felinity of his movements; the adolescent anxieties, still unfocused, still, as it were, with no fixed abode; the bouts of whinging, snivelling self-pity; the folksy tweediness of his country-boy Sunday-best suits which make you feel there must be a mouth-organ protruding from his hip pocket; the cigarette dangling from his lazy lower lip like a glow worm; above all, the way in which, playing a youth just released from prison (in *A Long Time Till Dawn*), and about to sling a brick through a storefront window, his gesture seemed instinctively to assume the pose of a nineteen-fifties movie poster. For it's that final example that perhaps best helps us to understand the secret of James Dean, the secret, too, of any actor or actress possessed of that famous *je ne sais quoi* question-beggingly known as 'star quality'.

Consider, for the moment, Fred Astaire. If one were to watch one of Astaire's musical-comedy numbers on a video recorder and press the freeze-frame button on any randomly selected frame, one would find the image thereby arrested and suspended to be of such impeccable physical grace and harmony that it could instantly serve as the jacket illustration of some expensive album on the history of the American cinema. I repeat, on *any* frame whatever.

Similarly with James Dean. Even in these early, often quite crudely staged telefilms, arresting the movement – which no NFT audience is able to do but which I frequently did during a private video screening – fatally produces a quintessential, archetypal image of the actor. Whether, as in *A Long Time Till Dawn*, he is pummelling his fists on a café table and impotently railing out at a hostile world ('You serve your time and you end up being branded for life!') or, in the same film, bewailing the fact of having been betrayed by a companion in whom he had placed his trust ('I thought you were my friend . . .') or, in *Glory in the Flower*, a William Inge play that was, as its title intimates, a pendant to *Splendor in the Grass* and was later filmed as *Bus Riley's Back in Town*, helplessly burying his face in his hands after a mortifying incident on a dance-hall floor ('I didn't do it on purpose – you don't have to blame me – everyone blames me!'), there he already was, from shot to shot, virtually from frame to frame, the cinema's poet of rage and humiliation.

That, surely, is what star quality is. A star may possess talent but, given the absolute consistency of image that is his gift to the screen, he ultimately does not need it. Or, more precisely, while an actor's talent has to be nurtured and developed, a star's is rather like a film's budget – it's useful to have a lot at one's disposal but a good director can perform wonders with surprisingly little. When he made these TV films James Dean was not necessarily a more talented actor than the other struggling unknowns one watches alongside him. But he alone was already, if as yet obscurely, a star.

Indecent exposures

The eighteenth-century aphorist Chamfort wrote somewhere that one would have to have swallowed three live toads for breakfast if one wished to be certain not to encounter anything more repulsive during the course of the morning. These days, with a copy of Kitty Kelley's biography of Nancy Reagan at hand, one can dispense with the toads.

Nancy Reagan is clearly a woman of no distinction whatsoever, a woman with a brain the size and colour of a small cancerous pea, and Kelley's biography of her, although quite naturally unputdownable, is nearly as sleazy as its subject. It is the sort of book that has one consulting its photographic illustrations time and time again simply to make a spot-check on the faces of the fascinatingly horrible individuals one has just been reading about. (Other, and far superior, examples of the same genre were James Fox's *White Mischief* and David McClintick's *Indecent Exposure*, an account of the David Begelman forged-cheque scandal in Hollywood.) But I read

Kelley's demolition job in (rather schizophrenic) tandem with another book whose concern was also with recent sociopolitical history, and it was the chasm between them, both in relation to the texts themselves and to their raw material, that was to prove so instructive.

The other book was French, Bernard-Henri Lévy's *Les Aventures de la liberté*, a racy, discursive chronicle (linked to a concurrent TV series) of the relationship between the Parisian intelligentsia and the twentieth century's major political convulsions, beginning with Zola's involvement in the Dreyfus case and concluding, in properly melancholy fashion, with that collective malediction of the seventies and early eighties that succeeded, like Tutankhamen's curse, in decimating an entire generation of intellectual *bonzes* (Sartre, Foucault, Barthes, Lacan, Althusser *et al*) within a single decade.

Lévy (something of a joke in certain quarters, one has to say) rose to prominence in the late seventies as one of the so-called *nouveaux philosophes* who anticipated – without, actually as Lévy himself does not shy from claiming, precipitating – the death throes of global Communist ideology by their then unorthodox contention that the Gulag was no mere aberration of Marxist practice but had always been as implicit in Marx's own theories as Auschwitz had been in Hitler's. And if, as metaphysics, his book is not precisely Kant's *Critique Of Pure Reason*, and is very seriously marred by its author's own self-aggrandising narcissism, it does impress me as a brilliant specimen of a kind of polemical journalism that barely exists over here.

These French intellectuals took some gruesomely wrong turnings in their political allegiances, they were often tainted by opportunism, by unconscious (and conscious) anti-semitism and even by a not always latent Fascism, with whose seductive trappings a handful of them 'flirted'. Yet it may be said of them, too, that they were concerned, genuinely, critically concerned, to engage at first hand with the history of ideas; and when they made mistakes (and it has been argued that many of them were 'right to be wrong' when they were, just as it has been argued that knee-jerk anti-

Communists were 'wrong to be right'), they paid for them in full, sometimes with their lives: Céline was ostracised, Drieu la Rochelle committed suicide, Brasillach was shot.

What one finds most startling, however, is the direct and for the most part congenial contact they were able to have with the politicians of the day. Claudel, Giraudoux and Saint-John Perse were all co-opted into the diplomatic service, Malraux was appointed De Gaulle's Minister of Culture, Régis Debray has long been a close associate of Mitterrand. And those who remained uninfluenceably hostile to the codified institutions of power were nevertheless often respectful of and friendly towards their representatives, whom they would meet on a basis of (near) equal footing.

It's true that a comparable (if incomparably less dazzling) tradition of intellectual dissidence existed in both Britain and the United States during the interwar years, but it has since almost completely atrophied. More to the point, considering the calibre of either nation's recent administrations, the notion of any reputable British or American thinker ideologically aligning him- or herself with the holders of supreme power is laughable. And even if a columnist is supposed to provide answers, I would like for once to pose a question, a no doubt stupid question to which I confess to having no ready answer. The question is this: Why, of late, have we elected such intellectual boobies?

Every village has its idiot, to be sure, but how could Americans twice elect Ronald Reagan President, the idiot of the global village? Why, instead of making joshingly coded allusions to his deficiencies, did no American journalist, not even those to whom his policies were anathema, ever call him a moron and be done with it? Why always the language of moderation with such an immoderately awful person?

And Thatcher? How could we have listened to her and not written her off once and for all as a dangerous buffoon, a better-educated Idi Amin Dada, our very own Idi Amin Mama? (When she offered her quaintly revisionist interpretation of the Good

Samaritan parable, one so wanted to be able to do what Woody Allen did with Marshall McLuhan in *Annie Hall* and suddenly confront her with Jesus.) Except in terms of the power she wielded, how could we take her pretentions even as half-seriously as we did?

And Bush, finally? Bush, who goes fishing while hundreds of thousands of Iraqi refugees starve? How can he live with that responsibility? I simply ask the question: How, realising what he has done, can he not want to kill himself? I would, and I'm no saint. But he goes fishing and turns his vacuous photo-opportunity smile on for the attendant cameramen. What does power do to these people? Does it lobotomise the soul?

Here is the news and here the newsreader

It was several years ago, on hearing on the *Nine O'clock News* that Jan Leeming had been mugged, that I first became alert to the self-referential paradox of newsreaders themselves featuring in news items. Leeming, quite badly bruised and doubtless still traumatised by the experience, was being interviewed in hospital by one of her own colleagues from the BBC News department, and she made what, given even circumstances as exceptional as these, seemed to me an extraordinarily ingenuous statement, something to the effect that 'I had no idea the world could be such a violent place.' Well, really, I remember saying to myself, she's been reading the news week after week, month after month – what sort of place did she think it was?

Subsequently, as I recall, another newsreader, also a woman but one whose name now escapes me, hit the tabloid headlines when she – wait for it now – actually found herself at a supermarket pay-out exit *with insufficient funds to pay for her purchases*. Yes, that was front-page news on the *Star* and the *Sun* and the *Mirror*. Inside, to be fair, and assuming you were prepared to track it down, there probably would have been some pithy this-is-basically-all-you-need-to-know-about-it sort of report (its sentences parading past the reader's eyes in single file, no more than one to a paragraph) on the other major event of the day in question: Reagan's Icelandic summit with Gorbachev.

Since those innocent days the market has opened up. Newsreaders, interviewers, presenters, commentators and even quiz show emcees with spangly microphones permanently brushing their lips like spangly udders, like so many showbiz dummy teats – all those, in short, whom we once regarded as neutral go-betweens, as near-invisible intermediaries – have themselves become stars as big as the stars they are paid to indulge and promote.

At the ICA Jonathan Ross interviews Lynn Barber on her own newly published collection of interviews, *Mostly Men*, and the ICA press handout complacently describes her as 'one of the most controversial and *newsworthy* interviewers of our time' (my emphasis). Kitty Kelley, author of the Nancy Reagan biography, is apparently to become the subject of a scurrilous biography in her turn. In a recent issue of the *Guardian* Catherine Bennett interviewed Brian Walden, himself a self-styled master of aggressive opinionation and interrogation. Media postmortems on the Gulf war tended to focus as much on those who reported it as those who fought it: broadcasters were metamorphosed into soldiers (can any serious history of the war afford to omit the tale of John Simpson and the smart bomb whizzing past the window of his hotel room?) while soldiers were metamorphosed into broadcasters (one thinks of all those retired Air Vice-Marshals who were retrieved from, and have now presumably been re-consigned to, mothballs). Just last week, too, Gavin Campbell, of the TV show *That's Life*, won a costly libel action against the newspaper *Today*, which had accused him of ruining an underwater wedding in Florida and vomiting over the presiding clergyman. (How, one wonders, is it possible to vomit underwater?)

And perhaps the whole evolutionary process of such bewildering self-referentiality can be most neatly plotted in four easy stages:

First, the news is news (e.g. the Afghanistan rebels).

Then, because the news is news, the newsreader becomes news (e.g. Sandy Gall becomes newsworthy by reporting on the Afghanistan rebels who themselves are newsworthy).

Then, because the newsreader is news, the news becomes news (e.g. the Afghanistan rebels become newsworthy because Sandy Gall reports on them).

Finally, the newsreader is news (and to hell with the Afghanistan rebels).

Speaking of the news, this year marks the fifth anniversay of the Chernobyl disaster (even if it may appear a touch premature, what with the extreme longevity of nuclear half-life, to be commemorating an event which will only truly be over in 25,000 years, give or take a millennium or two) and countless newspaper articles have been offering chilling descriptions of the damaged nuclear reactor, its corpses still emitting powerful radiation from the grave, its radioactive particles still seeping into the groundwater. I quote: 'the jagged, sooty silhouette of a factory disgorging its putrid fumes on to the sky and urinating unconcernedly into an oily, iridescent river'; 'its sole inhabitants some lonely, haunted dogs and an occasional bird or fish'; 'the sparse flowers which have begun to bloom again have no scent'; 'the grass is seen gently to undulate'.

That last, slightly too fantastical conceit gives the game away, I'm afraid. In reality, these stray phrases were extracted not from any article on Chernobyl but from a review (my own, as it happens) of the late Andrei Tarkovsky's film *Stalker*, which chronicled the journey undertaken by two disillusioned intellectuals to an abandoned rural area in the centre of the Soviet Union known only as 'the Zone' and to a mysterious Room at its core in which, it is claimed, one's every wish is granted. (The film leaves such a property unexplained, unless by its vague allusions to a meteorite that might once have crashed there.)

This year equally marks the anniversary of *Stalker*, but not the fifth, the tenth: Tarkovsky made it in 1981. In the same review from which I quote above I also wrote that the film's imagery had been 'rendered surrealistic by monochrome photography whose raspingly harsh textures suggest some grainy newsreel footage of the future'. *Some grainy newsreel footage of the future*. What seemed surrealistic has become realistic. What I interpreted as allegory has become fact. No matter when it was made, *Stalker* is an indictment of both Chernobyl and the whole nuclear nightmare and it ought to be re-released at once.

Killjoy was here

I recall, as a salacious adolescent, attempting with some school-chums to draw up the lengthiest possible list of synonyms for the sexual act. With the assistance of an ancient, much-thumbed dictionary of slang we contrived to unearth a startling number and variety, including such exotic items as 'giving somebody a thigh sandwich' and 'having bayonet practice'. But when we had wearied of our little pastime, it nevertheless continued to nag at me that at least one major synonym had been omitted. An hour later it occurred to me. The expression we had failed to include was 'making love'.

I thought of that omission when reading a recent piece in the *Guardian* by Nicholas de Jongh. De Jongh, who is currently writing a history of homosexuality in the theatre, was given access to the files of the Lord Chamberlain's office (which have lately been transferred from Buckingham Palace to the British Library), and his article is crammed with recommendations from various Chamberlains so preposterous one hardly knows whether to laugh or cry. Surely, one thinks, no sane person would wish to perpetuate a system which objected to a production of Sophocles's *Oedipus Rex* (in 1910!) as 'appealing to a vitiated public taste solely in the cause of indecency' or which, with reference to Peter Brook's anti-Vietnam show *US*, equated, as though they were virtual synonyms, the two descriptive adjectives 'beastly' and 'left-wing'. This institutionalised muzzling of expression – whose fundamentally castrating instincts and intentions are epitomised by a pithy instruction to the producer of John Osborne's *The Entertainer*: 'Omit "balls" ' – is surely totally indefensible.

And yet. In one variety or another, censorship *has* been defended over the years by poets and philosophers, from Goethe's 'And only law can give us freedom' (actually a defence of artistic self-discipline and self-denial) to the more perverse case of the late French philosopher Michel Foucault, who argued in his polemical study of sexuality that (to simplify grossly) every history of sex was also a history of repression, and that it was precisely centuries of repression by Church and State which had 'sexualised' mankind, which had erotically sensitised us all to the extent that we now know. Many, in addition, are the writers who have found it imperative to subject themselves to a degree of self-censorship in poetry and prose as a strictly formal or stylistic constraint, not unlike that of the sonnet or the alexandrine or the Aristotelian unities, in the conviction that such a constraint will serve as a spur to subtlety and invention.

That, arguably, used to be true of the classic American cinema, which, from the early thirties to the late sixties, was corseted in the so-called Hays Code (named after its formulator, Will H. Hays), a self-regulatory charter of rights and wrongs in matters pertaining particularly to sex. The Code held, notably, that 'sex perversion or any inference [*sic*] to it is forbidden' and that 'seduction or rape should never be more than suggested'.

Now, any institution that felt it necessary to prohibit Ronald Reagan from saying 'razzberries' in *Bedtime for Bonzo* and insisted that W. C. Fields cut 'Nuts to you!' from *The Bank Dick* had clearly lost touch with the society it had been set up to protect. The problem, though, is that where once 'seduction or rape' could merely be suggested, the dissolution of the Code has tended to mean that in the contemporary American cinema the idea of 'suggestion' has become almost as much of a taboo as once was explicit expression. It's as though there has been a direct and implacable transposition from 'You *can't* show it!' to 'You *must* show it!' What the Hays Code did for Hollywood was oblige its writers and directors to devise another and more purely aesthetic code – in the sense that the films themselves were coded, so to speak, and had therefore to be deciphered. And by no means all of the consequences were negative ones. A delicious ambiguity pervades a lot of movies from that period. Is Barbara Stanwyck a prostitute or just a girl out for a good time, we ask ourselves while watching a typically sombre *film noir* of the forties? Has Cary Grant already gone to bed with Irene Dunne, we fall to musing in the course of some shiny romantic comedy, or is their flirtation still platonic? Are we really supposed to understand that Jean Arthur and Joel McCrea are not sleeping together? They can't be, we feel, yet equally they *must* be.

These questions – oddly similar to ones we tend to pose about our everyday acquaintances – had the effect of creating a sort of parallel world, an absurd world in many ways, in which married couples invariably slept in twin beds and effeminate butlers were never suspected of entertaining telegraph boys below stairs, but a world, too, which possessed its own peculiar and not unsexy charm. In the word 'suggest' there is after all an implication of suggestiveness.

In any event, great directors thrived on the Hays Code. Hitchcock, precisely because he never succeeded in breaching the cool, inviolate exteriors of his frosty blonde heroines, was responsible for some of the most sheerly erotic sequences ever filmed. By concealing Marlene Dietrich behind furs, feathers and shadowy lattice-work veils, Josef von Sternberg managed to arouse audiences for whom the fact of concealment alone generated the requisite excitement, just as for the fetishist the garter belt becomes more significant than the leg it encircles. (That garter belt is a perfect metaphor for old Hollywood's fundamental *perversity*.) And in the famous 'Walls of Jericho' sequence of *It Happened One Night*, when Clark Gable and Claudette Colbert are forced to share a single motel room, Frank Capra came up with what was in essence a marvellous parody of Hays Code regulations.

Nowadays, of course, these characters would not only sleep together but sleep in the nude. Which is, I suppose, an improvement – except that nudity can also be a uniform, a straitjacket. One need not be a prude about four-letter words (or four-letter images) to entertain a certain nostalgia, even regret, for the bad, repressed old days when, instead of giving each other 'a thigh sandwich' or 'having bayonet practice', instead of (for let us not be censors ourselves) *fucking*, the characters in Hollywood movies actually, if discreetly, 'made love'.

The mother of all battleaxes

Sailor Beware! Few, for me, are the titles that carry so potently evocative a charge as that of Philip King and Falkland Cary's vintage farce, currently being revived at the Lyric Hammersmith. Its original production, staged as long ago as 1955, was the very first I ever saw in a professional theatre; and I have only to close my eyes to see it still, to see Peggy Mount as Emma Hornett rampaging through its chintzy front-room set and hear her bellowing 'Henreeee!' and (ultimately a literal statement of fact, in view of the play's then record-breaking run) 'If I've said it once, I've said it a thousand times . . .'

I saw the film version, too, with Cyril Smith as Mount's hen-pecked, ferret-breeding husband, his moustache permanently adroop like the moue of the mask of tragedy; Shirley Eaton as the bride-to-be (also named Shirley, as, precociously starstruck as I was, I remember thoughtfully noting); Ronald Lewis as her sailor groom, Albert Tuffnell; a very youthful Gordon Jackson as Albert's Scottish best man, Carnoustie, shimmying not unsexily out of his bell-bottoms; and – last but, if least, then only in the physical sense – the sublime Esma Cannon (note to the National Film Theatre: when an *hommage à* Esma Cannon?) as the family's resident poor relation, a tiny, shrivelled, mousy flutter of a woman who was forever depositing hot teapots on Emma's varnished sideboard and who, upon learning that Shirley had been jilted at the altar just as she herself had been forty years before (it was her tirelessly rehearsed 'great sorrow'), squeaked out what was to be the play's single most memorable line: 'It's a curse, I tell you, a curse on the house of Hornett!'

Prima inter pares, of course, was Peggy Mount herself, a postcard by Donald McGill teased into reverberant life, a Gorgon with curlers instead of serpents in her hair, the Mother Courage of mothers-in-law and the Bernhardt of the back-to-backs. Mount's Emma Hornett was a statue carved out of a single slab of stone, a Mount Rushmore that she had all to herself; it was the role of a lifetime and she played it to the hilt and well beyond. There is, in fact, a curious steroscopic effect that tends to operate between a performer and the role in which he or she has been cast. If he or she should chance to be miscast, one's eye (or one's mind's eye) will continue to register the two discrete personae of role and performer as remaining fuzzily distinct from one another. If, however, as with Peggy Mount in *Sailor Beware*, the overlap is total, if there strikes one as an absolute coincidence of role and performer, then the character and the actress will fuse into one and the effect is of a praeternaturally vivid three-dimensionality. It scarcely matters whether the performer in question is a great actress; what is important is that she is the right actress.

In the Lyric Hammersmith revival the role has been taken by Jane Freeman, who is perhaps best-known for her appearances as a tearoom proprietress in *Last of the Summer Wine*, and she makes a persuasive enough battleaxe (as such wives used to be called). But just as Richard III will always belong to Olivier, so Emma Hornett will always belong to Peggy Mount.

I could go on endlessly celebrating the lowbrow splendours of this magnificent farce. (For a postmodern aesthete, brows and classes are exactly alike: high or low, anything but the dreaded middle.) But the question imposes as to why, within the iconographic parameters of what might be called the British *commedia dell'arte*, the mother-in-law has come to assume so central and irreplaceable a position. In the history of the French farce, by contrast, the primary figure has always been the *cocu*, or cuckold, a word that possesses no particular mythic connotations for the English. Indeed, where in France it's even now a fairly common term of abuse, I wonder whether not a few ordinary people in this country would be obliged to reflect for a moment or two before being able to say what it means.

Yet the British tradition is perhaps not as all too Britishly sexless as might at first appear to be the case. The cuckold and the mother-in-law do after all have one crucial function in common: each implies the insinuation of an alien body inside a marriage. One might even argue that, in a British farce, the husband finds himself cuckolded by his wife's mother, not lover, just as the mother-in-law's resentment and frustration initially derive from having had her daughter abducted from her by her son-in-law and thus from having been 'cuckolded' herself. And the ostensibly diametric opposition of these two national and even ethnic stereotypes, one (the French) founded on sexual desire, the other (the British) on an exacerbated maternal possessiveness, would be dissolved even further if one were to interpret *Sailor Beware* as the articulation of an inverted Oedipus (an Oedipa Regina, if you like) in which a mother's repressed craving to 'kill' her son (-in-law) and 'marry' her daughter causes her to –

Ah, basta! You may have to open up a clock to understand how it works, but it's the surface of its dial that you consult if you simply want to know what time it is. When the curtain rises on *Sailor Beware* at the Lyric Hammersmith the time is 1955 and what the play retrieves is a precise, lost moment of British cultural history.

Authors and auteurs

I have often thought that, if it is ever to reinvent itself, what the literary establishment of this country needs is a *politique des auteurs* for writers; for the Author, in short, to be considered as Auteur.

The so-called *politique des auteurs* – or, as it came to be known in English-speaking parts, the Auteur Theory – was formulated in Paris in the early nineteen-fifties by a group of regular contributors to the film critical journal *Cahiers du Cinéma* who would eventually graduate to filmmaking themselves: they were, most famously, Jean-Luc Godard, François Truffaut, Eric Rohmer, Jacques Rivette and Claude Chabrol. For these young Turks of Parisian cinéphilia it was the director rather than the scenarist whom one had to regard as a film's 'author', who would brand his sensibility on to its every shot like a logo on the hip pocket of a pair of hip jeans; and the collective achievement of the Hollywood directors whom they especially adulated (Hitchcock, Hawks, Sternberg, Lang, Welles, etc.) offered conclusive proof that it was possible for wholly personal works of art to emerge from within an adamantine capitalist, indeed industrialo-corporate system. As I once wrote in *Sight and Sound*: 'At its best the Hollywood product was to teach them, first as critics, then as filmmakers, an invaluable lesson in economy of means, generosity of sentiment and elegance of performance, much the same virtues as an earlier Ecole de Paris

– the Impressionists – had assimilated from the Japanese printmakers.' However debased it has since become, with every director now treated an an *auteur* from practically his (or her) very first film, the theory can claim to have had the salutary effect of radically reforming the way all of us, filmmakers, critics and ordinary spectators alike, think about the cinema.

I suggest above that a similar critical approach might well be instrumental in revitalising the way we think about literature – which of course immediately raises the question of how one can circularly graft back on to one discipline a theory for which that discipline represents the referential model? Since the term *auteur* was specifically designed to draw a productive analogy between the filmmaker and the writer, surely re-applying it to writers would be a redundancy? And, particularly in the wake of, and wake for, the Death of the Author, can anyone really imagine a clique of literary critics electing to call themselves, after the Hitchcocko-Hawksians of *Cahiers du Cinéma*, the Burgesso-Brooknerians, let's say?

Well, the world has moved on, and not only for the cinema. In view of the intellectual respectability that films (certain types of film, that is) are at long last enjoying, in view of the fact that the medium has finally begun to command serious attention from an intelligentsia that was once contemptuous of its presumption to be treated as an art form among others, the public images of cinema and literature have started increasingly to coincide. Literature in this country, after all, has its quota of good, or goodish, mainstream fiction, virtually identical in its mimetic linearity and basic formal conservatism to the higher-minded examples of the cinema's current output. It has its cheap and cheerful genre novels, ignored by the majority of reviewers just as Hollywood westerns and thrillers used to be. It has its 'brand name' commercial blockbusters, from Shirley Conran to Bret Easton Ellis, replete with what is described in the cinema as 'product placement'. It has its 'art novels', as we say 'art movies'. In the Booker Prize ceremony, it even has its Oscar night.

But if literary criticism tends still to be rather more intelligent and literate than most film reviewing, what it conspicuously lacks, and conspicuously wants, is a quality that continues to inform even the feeblest and most unlettered of film reviews – a willingness, frankly, to cut through the crap, a sense of passionate partisanship, of *this but not that*.

What is required is the aggressive sort of critic capable of making elegantly chopped mincemeat out of all those well-intentioned and ultimately styleless artefacts which currently pass for serious literature – analogous to the academic films of William Wyler and Fred Zinnemann and Sam Wood that were prominent in Hollywood's Pantheon until the Auteur Theory swept its cobwebs away. (Since it would be craven of me not to name names, let me propose William Boyd and Penelope Lively as choice specimens. Has anyone ever been able to detect a William Boyd style? Or recognise a Penelope Lively sentence? Both are authors but is either an *auteur*?) Critics, too, who will champion a favourite writer with a passion no less vigorous, even one who suffers under the gross disadvantage of living abroad. (A purely subjective choice again, but I think of the Paris-based Hungarian, and slightly misleadingly named, Agota Kristof, whose twinned novels *The Notebook* and *The Proof*, published in Britain by Methuen, impress me as near-masterpieces.)

In the book pages of any self-respecting newspaper or magazine a new work of fiction by William Boyd or Penelope Lively is passed under review at a length and with a gravity that will, I'm convinced, bemuse posterity. Kristof, if reviewed at all, has almost invariably found herself tucked away under Other New Novels or else, *quel horreur!*, Translated Fiction. And comparable injustices on both sides of the tracks are not far short of legion.

'*Vive Hitchcock! A bas Wyler!*' – that was the auteurists' rallying cry. '*Vive Kristof! A bas Lively!*' – that would be mine. Actually, though, what is important is not so much the choice of names itself as the '*Vive*' and the '*A bas*'. A little factionism, a little *ferocity*, if you please, reviewers.

Outing *Grandstand*

There exists a newfashioned practice in the United States termed 'outing', whereby homosexuals, usually celebrities, who have elected not to publicise their sexuality may find themselves forcibly exposed by their more militant confrères. It is, to say the least, a questionable method of fostering sexual tolerance and liberation, but the principle, if applied to some less contentious spheres of human activity, strikes me as a valid one nevertheless. Thus it gives me no small measure of pleasure to 'out' John Philips, the editor of BBC1's *Grandstand*, as a philistine.

Since, with a single exception, sport holds no great interest for me, I watched one recent *Grandstand* programme solely for its coverage of the final of the French Open tennis tournament. Although I am not impervious to the by now anachronistic charm of Wimbledon's grass-court championship, and would not suggest that the matches played at the Roland Garros stadium are systematically more thrilling and elegant, yet I do believe that the dreary serve-and-volley, hit-and-run finals which have lately been the rule in this country are practically impossible on a clay surface. And this theory of mine was confirmed by the first two sets disputed by Agassi and Courier, which, if scarcely classics of their kind, were paced by the extended rallies which at Wimbledon have become a thing of the past. In short, if not quite biting my nails, I was totally absorbed.

Now, it is true that the British have always been famously shy of those theoretical methodologies that, like V1 rockets, come regularly whizzing across the Channel. Yet one of the most recent of them, semiology, might be made to appear less terroristically rebarbative than it does if it were demonstrated, for example, that a term like 'signifier' can easily be related to the text-book grammatical trope of synecdoche, or 'the part for the whole'. Lecturing at the Collège de France, Barthes was once mischievously asked by a student what the signifier of a lecturer was; after an instant of reflection, he simply pointed to the carafe of water and upturned tumbler which stood on the table in front of him. Likewise, while filming a *Late Show* segment, precisely on Barthes, in a local bistro called 'Le Dôme', I was asked by one of the crew members whether I thought the café had an emblematic signifier and proposed 'emôD eL' – which is to say, 'Le Dôme' backwards, the way one reads its painted window-sign from within the premises and which I felt captured the quintessence of a certain 'café experience'. And, the other day, while watching the Royal Ballet's current, mildly gorgeous revival of Nijinska's and Poulenc's *Les Biches*, I came to realise the extent to which the iconography of the nineteen-twenties, of which this particular ballet is an exemplary artefact, has been reduced to a set of chic signifiers, the most prominent of which is undoubtedly the cigarette-holder. Wherever you find an elongated cigarette holder, and whatever the context, there will always be a distinct whiff of the twenties.

Yes, yes, you finally manage to interrupt, that's all very interesting, but what on earth has it got to do with *Grandstand's* coverage of the French Open? The answer is: nothing, absolutely nothing.

I might claim, to be sure, that this is after all an article on the arts and that, in both of its thematic strands, television and semiology, art of one description or another is at issue. I am not so foolish, though, as to suppose that a reader who started reading it because of an *a priori* interest in televised sport (or even in 'outing' on the American gay scene) will inevitably be prepared to follow me into a lengthy digression on the detection and elucidation of cultural signifiers. Yet that was exactly the arbitrary, take-it-or-leave-it attitude of which *Grandstand* was guilty. After two sets of the Agassi-Courier match, with tension building up nicely and without, as they say, so much as a by-your-leave, BBC1 suddenly switched the programme's – and, by extension, the hapless viewer's – attention to the First Test between England and the West Indies, which had earlier been rained off. (If the British were to devise a sport which *had* to be played in the rain, our national climate would pick up dramatically.)

The presumption underlying such a decision must be that, if one is interested in one sport, one ought logically to be interested in all sports, to be interested in, as it were, 'sport'. That there are people with such catholic enthusiasms I don't deny – yet, unless they believe diversification to be a virtue in and of itself, I find it hard to imagine that even they appreciate having the *narrative* of an event, any event, quite so brutally fragmented. One can, after all, be interested in music and be listening to a concert on the radio and yet resent having the first two movements of a Bruckner symphony brusquely interrupted by, let's say, the *Rhapsody in Blue*; or in film without necessarily feeling in the mood, after an hour of Bresson's *Au hasard, Balthazar*, for a Busby Berkeley production number from *42nd Street*; or in an article on *Grandstand* without being at all minded to read about the latest production of the Royal Ballet.

The BBC's attitude strikes me as a very definition of philistinism. And with its ecstatic trailers reeling off an entire evening's schedule in the (perhaps well-founded) confidence that viewers will perceive some kind of delirious continuity in a chat show, a sitcom, the *Nine O'clock News*, a made-for-TV message movie, *Newsnight* and *The Late Show*, thereby wholly abdicating their prerogative of selection, it would also appear to be what much of television programming is currently predicated on. It's possible, indeed, to regard TV's sports coverage as a neat signifier and synecdoche of the medium's whole philistine discourse.

Internationalities

The European cinema, we know, is currently in crisis. Attendances in western Europe have been falling off steadily year after year; or else, if rising (as happens to be the case in the United Kingdom, once regarded, cinematically speaking, as the continent's ingrowing toenail), the rise can mostly be attributed to the perennial popularity of the American product, which even in France, with its real and still fully functioning national cinema, has succeeded in routing most of the local competition. In eastern Europe the situation is even more calamitous, as a consequence not only of the sudden, quota-free pervasion of Hollywood movies but also of the no less sudden withdrawal – during a tumultuous period of transition from a centrally controlled to a market-based economy – of the state subsidies on which filmmakers used entirely to depend.

As two symptomatic indicators of the pass to which the crisis has come, reflect that:

One, whereas 'difficult' European filmmakers could once at least count on the international festival circuit for the kind of exposure and prestige that their work needs if it is to attract a sizeable public, the Palme d'Or at Cannes has been awarded for the last three successive years to an American film (Steven Soderbergh's *sex, lies and videotape*, David Lynch's *Wild at Heart* and, this year, the Coen Brothers' *Barton Fink*).

Two, it now tends to be perceived of Europe, as used to be true exclusively of the Third World, that no country can be expected to boast more than one major filmmaker at any given time. Thus Spain has its Pedro Almodóvar, Finland has its Aki Kaurasmäki, Poland its Krzysztof Kieslowski, Greece its Theo Angelopoulos, Portugal its Mañoel de Oliveira, Denmark its Lars von Trier, Britain its Peter Greenaway. (As that final example demonstrates, these are, for anyone who has seen and admired the films of Mike

Leigh, Terence Davies and Bill Forsyth, vague, ill-informed extrapolations rather than verifiable statements of fact.)

There does exist, though, an area in which a handful of European filmmakers have mined a vein of international success, inventing in the process a whole new aesthetico-sociological 'genre'. This genre, if that is in fact what it is, would comprise such recent hits as Claude Berri's *Jean de Florette* and *Manon des Sources* (plus his very latest, *Uranus*, an adaptation not of Pagnol but of another literary Marcel, Aymé); Jean-Paul Rappeneau's *Cyrano de Bergerac*, a phenomenally money-making superproduction; Yves Robert's *La Gloire de mon père*, which has only just opened here, and its sequel, about to be released, *Le Château de ma mère*, both of them also adapted from Pagnol; and, out of E. M. Forster, James Ivory's *A Room with a View* and *Maurice*, and Charles Sturridge's *Where Angels Fear to Tread*. (With Ivory's adaptation of *Howards End* now in preparation the sole Forster novel to remain unfilmed is *The Longest Journey*. If the rights to it are ever sold, the cycle will at last be complete and screenwriters may well be set to devising pastiche plots just as the writers of the Bond films did when they had exhausted the original Fleming canon.)

That may appear a bizarrely diverse line-up of cultural glories – Pagnol, Aymé, Rostand, Forster – to be encompassed within a single 'genre', even one held between the fastidiously sceptical tweezers of quotation marks. Yet what all of these writers have in common is that they have inspired films *whose subject matter is their own nationality*.

Consider those made in France. Even if no one could ever accuse *Jean de Florette* and *Manon des Sources* of being underplotted, the tautological message that they are ultimately designed to emit is that of their own indelible Frenchness, of what Barthes would have called their 'francity'. Or *toujours Provence*, as one says *toujours l'amour*. To be fair, and hard as it is to assess this in retrospect, there *was* a genuine commercial risk attached to reinventing Pagnol for the eighties, as Berri did: such rather dated, fusty material was by no means self-evidently commercial. Berri's gamble paid off more than handsomely, however, and the rest, as they say, is history (or, rather, geography). Yves Robert's films, on the other hand, cannot any longer claim to be rehabilitating an unjustly ignored author. They are third-generation cribs, copies of copies, which have at least the cynical merit of clearly laying their cards on the table by dispensing with narrative altogether and indulging the spectator in a delirium of pure evocation. Aren't the French French? is what *La Gloire de mon père* and *Le Château de ma mère* seem to be saying, and all they seem to be saying. The Provençal countryside, filmed with such unaffected *naturel* by Pagnol himself in the thirties and forties, obligingly sits up and poses for Robert; and Marseilles is reduced to the cosiest of caricatures, a Mediterranean city where all the *garçons* are *garçons de café* and all the *filles* are *filles de joie.*

As for Forster, until *A Passage to India* was adapted by David Lean and *A Room With a View* more or less simultaneously by Ivory, he probably struck the film industry, insofar as it thought about him at all, as much too bookish a novelist for so voraciously populist a medium. But times change, and attitudes with them, and Forster has come to provide the ideal cultural alibi for a strain of 'Georgian' cinema (on the model of Georgian poetry) whose principal function is to preserve, not the present *status quo*, but the last *status quo* but one; to make us regret an eternally retarded *status quo ante* of nonpareil elegance and graciousness, regret it not because we have 'lost' it but because we never had it.

The irony is that this newfound flair for national self-promotion is a lesson learned from . . . where else but Hollywood. As film historians have agreed since nearly the turn of the century, the primary source of the American cinema's strength, whatever the period, the studio or the genre, has always been that the fundamental theme of its films is, either latently or overtly, what it means to be American.

Did the Gulf war really take place?

The other day I had an oddly Proustian little epiphany: on little more than a whim, while dozily rousing myself from bed, I switched on breakfast television. What was so Proustian about that? The fact that it instantly conjured up for me the sole period of my life when I regularly watched television in the early morning, a period when 'the news' also worked on night-shift – the Gulf war. And as I experienced my nostalgic revelation, I recalled an anecdote related somewhere by Cocteau. In 1919 or thereabouts he encountered an elderly newspaper vendor selling copies of *Le Figaro* at twice the standard price. His curiosity piqued, Cocteau duly purchased a copy, only to discover that it was two years out-of-date. When he protested, the newspaper vendor cannily replied, 'But, *cher monsieur*, that's precisely why it's more expensive – *because there's still the war in it.*'

Is 'nostalgia' a legitimate reaction to the memory of a conflict in which tens, possibly hundreds, of thousands of lives were sacrificed, even if that same conflict also allowed those of us secure in the West to live for a few months at an unaccustomedly heightened level of intensity? Is it legitimate to 'miss' a period in which the news itself actually made news, in which we found ourselves held in thrall, night after night, morning after morning, to the 1001 tales of Saddam (or Scheherasaddam)? Is it legitimate to refer to some event of the recent past, as I have already found myself doing, as having occurred, not 'before the Gulf war', but simply, bluntly, 'before the war', as though my own generation finally, gratefully, had a first-hand war to call its own?

There being surely nothing more revolting than a *nostalgie de boue* for war, for a war at least in which one was not called upon to fight, one trusts that the answer to each of these questions would be negative. But what if the war in question were not a 'real' one? For that is the premise of a new book by Jean Baudrillard, the Pope of postmodernism and the theorist of the hyperreal.

La Guerre du Golfe n'a pas eu lieu (an obvious parody of Giraudoux's *La Guerre de Troie n'aura pas lieu*) is composed of three essays: 'The Gulf War Will Not Take Place' (which originally appeared in *Libération* and was translated for and reprinted in the *Guardian*); 'The Gulf War Is Not Really Taking Place' (originally published in *Libération*); and 'The Gulf War Did Not Take Place' (written for book publication only). And Baudrillard's thesis is that the Gulf war was merely the simulacrum of a war ('simulacrum': one of the key words of postmodernism); its 'televisual subterfuge'; a war that was made, as one now makes love, with condoms; a war that was not declared, not fought and not truly won; as much of a 'real' war as a football match whose final score was 100,000 against 150 or so would be regarded as a real football match.

There are some brilliant *aperçus* in this book. The notion, for example, of the Gulf war constantly, neurotically, scrutinising its image in the mirror of the TV screen (without which incentive, Baudrillard implies, it would not have been waged at all), repeatedly asking itself: 'Am I beautiful enough, am I operational enough, spectacular enough, sophisticated enough, to take my place in the history of warfare?' The notion of that poor, helpless, oil-caked comorant – which we TV viewers were shown again and again as though it were the war's logo, its registered trademark – as the symbol of our own impotence when confronted with such a gummily unintelligible event. The notion, most vertiginously, that what was ultimately at stake was not political or territorial domination, as with a 'real' war, but the very status of war itself, its meaning and its future.

Yet, reading his book on the sunlit terrace of a Parisian café, I have to say that I became more and more sensitive to the glee, the faintly chilling gusto, with which Baudrillard seemed to be pouncing on this, the first of the 'hyperreal wars', as he perceives it, almost as though he *needed* such a war to vindicate his theories of postmodernism just as the Pentagon needed it to vindicate all its glossy weaponry. And his concluding argument, that the Gulf war's victims were not 'real' cadavers, was enough to turn even me into a bluff Johnsonian pragmatist.

And then it happened. Distractedly turning a page, I spilt some red wine on my white linen jacket and, aghast at the stain it had made, I confess that for a moment or two I didn't give a damn about the war or the cormorant or the tens (or even hundreds) of thousands dead.

Stains are like that. They have the capacity suddenly to draw one's own petty little existence into outlandish close-up, they force one to acknowledge that the world – the world *before* the stain – was maybe not quite as ugly and beastly a place as one had imagined. For now, to contend with, alas, there is both the world *and* the stain.

And if one must go scouting, Baudrillard-fashion, for metaphors, it might make better and more modest sense to regard the Gulf war as nothing other than a stain on the world. One reacts to it violently at first, in the belated realisation of just how comfortable one was after all with the pre-stain world. One endeavours to erase it with some 'wonder' product ('New Improved World Order', perhaps), which, however, usually succeeds only in spreading it. Then, little by little, one learns to live with it until, as with every other stain the world has sustained, one ends by barely noticing it.

It's a strange thing, though. I would not dream of wearing a jacket as stained as the world is, yet I do manage to live in that world, day after day, contentedly enough.

The 'the' and the 'and'

Recently, during a weekend at a friend's cottage in the country, I chanced to be reading *Pride and Prejudice* (I have always thought it rather vulgar to refer to one's 're-reading' a classic, even if it should be true) when my friend's other guest, a New Yorker, ambled over to my deckchair, glanced at the jacket of my book and remarked in his native city's best smart-alecky style, '*Pride and Prejudice*, eh? Sounds like some bestselling bodice-ripper about the love of a cotton planter for a beautiful mulatress in the antebellum South.'

For once I found myself unhobbled by my chronic *esprit d'escalier*. 'Actually,' I replied. 'I don't agree. For if such a novel did exist, as I'm sure it does, it wouldn't be called "Pride and Prejudice" but "*The* Pride and *the* Prejudice". And it just now strikes me,' I added pompously, 'that these two redundant direct articles epitomise what Wilde said about our two countries being separated by a common language.'

Rather neat, I felt; indeed, the rejoinder quite made my day. It also set me to wondering, however, whether I had been not only witty but actually right. This 'The Something and the Something' form of title, often rendered even more crudely antithetical by some very elementary alliteration, is most usually to be found in (bad) films – *The High and the Mighty, The Bad and the Beautiful, The Proud and the Profane, The Pride and the Passion*. Yet the political journalist David Halberstam called his best-known book *The Best and the Brightest*, Scott Fitzgerald just missed entering the lists with *The Beautiful and Damned*, and even Faulkner couldn't resist naming his finest novel, not *Sound and Fury*, as the Shakespearean reference prompted him to do, but *The Sound and the Fury*. And the question which then began to exercise me was no longer whether these redundancies constituted a specifically American quirk but whether it was at all possible to attribute to a basic semantic prop like 'the' a secondary, subtextual layer of meaning, a *connotation*.

(In this respect it might be worth recalling that Mary McCarthy once accused Lillian Hellman of perjuring herself with every word she said, including 'the' and 'and'.)

Let's try it out, anyway. One is probably intended to interpret the 'the' of these titles as the signifier of some species of the Ideal, no doubt pseudo-Platonic in its pretension but all too rapidly debased and trivialised in its expression. Thus, in *The Bad and the Beautiful*, an amusing second-rate film by Vincente Minnelli about the glamorous rapacity of Hollywood in the nineteen-fifties, what such a title implies is that its characters, who at a first, superficial glance would seem to be bitching and backbiting in the purest soap-opera fashion, should instead be seen as belonging to a higher, cod-Nietzschean Pantheon of emblematic archetypes whose actions, situated beyond good and evil, have been emancipated from the mean-spirited polities of middle-class morality. That at any rate is the idea. Considering, however, the wellnigh unbridgeable abyss between that latent ambition and the undistinguished film which has been saddled with it, the result, by far the most frequent one in these cases, is what I would term the fallacy of the Bathetic Absolute.

So much, then, for 'the'. Could 'and', too, I now wondered, be made to generate some underlying, connotational meaning of its own? I considered this characteristic sentence from Hemingway's short story 'My Old Man':

I'd go ahead of him when we hit the road and I could run pretty good and I'd look around and he'd be jogging easy just behind me and after a little while I'd look around again and he'd begun to sweat.

No fewer than five 'ands' in forty-two words: a little under an eighth of the sentence. And they are so important (particularly for a parodist) to the way in which we receive that sentence, the way in which it resonates in our inner and indeed outer ear, that, paradoxically, it becomes the simple, almost *faux-naïf* phrases held between them that strike the reader as 'connectives'. These reiterated 'ands', with their faint but audible hint of Biblical rhetoric ('And the whole earth was of one language, and of one speech'), are patently meant to function as ennobling agents in Hemingway's dripping-tap prose. They are designed to archetypify the story's outwardly seedy characters, to persuade us that there is something about them slightly more elemental than their deceptively modest personalities appear at first to suggest, that in their very inarticulacy there may be detected certain mute but surely eternal verities.

Does there, then, exist such a thing as a word without a meaning – or, rather, without an ulterior meaning? Or even part of a word? Might it not prove a valuable and interesting exercise to investigate the cryptic implications of what might be called linguistic chromaticism – such lexical 'chords', so to speak, as 'tz', as in 'Ritz', 'glitz' and 'blitz', or 'sn', as in 'sneer', 'snake', 'snore', 'snarl'? Or even as basic a punctuational unit as a colon, a comma or a pair of inverted commas? Or is it all strictly stylistic? Ah, the sense and the sensibility!

Show business

There is a pleasurably excruciating moment in *Roger and Me*, Michael Moore's award-winning documentary film on his attempts to confront Roger Smith, the President of General Motors, with the human consequences of GM's closure of its plants in Flint, Michigan. Moore is interviewing the simpering, limp-wristed stage manager of the local variety theatre, who is interrupted in his fulsome eulogies to the big stars who have played there (most of them, as one cannot help remarking, has-beens: Peggy Lee, Pat Boone, etc.) by a noisy offscreen thud. 'Oh God,' he squeals at the bemused Moore with hand-wringing self-satisfaction, 'you gotta excuse all this craziness backstage!'

Excuse it? What he really means is: Don't you just *love* it! Isn't show business just so deliriously nutty! Yet poignant, too, in its fashion, bravely shrugging off its own heartaches in its relentless determination to make all you lovely folks out there forget yours.

The American industrial hinterland may be spiralling into terminal decline, half the community of Flint and once prosperous cities like it may be out of work – as long as show business survives, as long as the unemployed can hear Peggy Lee singing the same weary old standards that she has been trading in for practically half-a-century, there can't be too much wrong with the world. But then, for those who labour in the lush vineyards of the entertainment industry, there is no such thing as 'people' – there is only 'the public'.

Which is why, in spite of my indifference to her as a performer, and in spite of its mediocrity purely as film, I found the experience of watching another documentary, Alek Keshishian's *In Bed With Madonna*, so very bracing. Not that Madonna doesn't, in her own peculiarly garish style, incarnate many of show business's time-worn values and attitudes. But she does at least take a scythe to all its self-serving hypocrisy, as witness her on-camera putdown of poor, hapless Kevin Costner, and clearly doesn't give a hoot for all its codified do's and don't's. (She seems to take a positive delight in looking drab and sweaty.) She herself, in short, is a backstage thud, a one-woman repository of noises off.

Madonna and I have something in common: we both *abominate* traditional show business. For my own part, I hate just about everything that the accursed expression connotes. I hate the smiles that appear to have been glazed on to showbiz faces, smiles akin to that of the wretched hero of Victor Hugo's *The Man Who Laughs*, his lips surgically slashed into a permanent crescent moon of hilarity so that funfair patrons can chuck rotten eggs at him in the secure knowledge that he will always be a good sport. How they do smile, these showbiz troupers! An unsmiling Bob Monkhouse, say, is a totally unimaginable concept, a real mind-boggler. It's almost as though, instead of frowning, he smiled once as an infant, the direction of the wind changed and the smile was to remain forever after jammed on his waxy features. Even more than the smiles, though, I hate the tears. Oh, those tears that show business personalities keep on apparently uninterrupted tap for awards ceremonies, gala benefits, Oscar nights and the like – those tears that glitter on their powdery cheeks like so many miniature paste gems from Ratner's and are probably worth not much more than a pair of Ratner's earrings are. (I have sometimes fantasised about devising new lyrics for Andrew Lloyd Webber's best-known ballad: 'Don't Cry For Me, Att-en-bor-ough!').

But what I hate most of all are the emblematic props of show business, those time-warped props that now look hardly less fossilised than the red noses, baggy pants and flapping, open-toed shoes of a circus clown. Shirley MacLaine's top hat, for example (its stiff brim rakishly rapped rat-a-tat against the back of her head as she makes her grimacing exit from the stage), her sheer waist-high black tights and her silvery, spangly cane. Or the late (or, in showbiz patois, late, *great*) Sammy Davis Jr's natty black bowler, shiny black silk suit, gaudy Paisley waistcoat and neat little pumps, pumps so glossy you could have removed a cinder from your eye in their reflection. And of course the prop that is shared by all of them, the microphone – that microphone that, even before they open their mouths, has begun to convey the message that they are yet again about to belt their hearts out and bend our ears back, that microphone whose wire they will yank behind them from time to time with *exactly* the same gesture we pathetic mortals have to make when tugging the wiring of a vacuum cleaner to circumvent an awkward corner.

Show business, it's perhaps worth pointing out, is not a universal, therefore not an inevitable, phenomenon. Its influence may be felt in France, Germany and Italy, its slick conventions may be clumsily imitated in Eastern Europe, the Middle East and beyond (only in show business is slickness regarded as a virtue), but it remains an essentially American tradition. By a kind of vicarious brain drain in which the individual stays behind and only his brain departs, showbiz Britons simply and laboriously imitate their American counterparts.

Thus they have learned never to refer to Shirley Bassey or Carol Channing as a woman, always as a lady (as in 'a great lady' or 'one feisty lady'). They have learned to be ready at the drop of a (top) hat to perform that elementary soft-shoe shuffle, the absolute zero degree of choreographic artistry, in which the feet are as indolently twiddled as thumbs, but which is nevertheless a basic, obligatory qualification for induction into the big, happy showbiz family. They have learned above all that, even if the heart is breaking, *especially* if the heart is breaking, they must smile, smile, smile!

Now I realise how Scrooge felt during the rest of the year. Bah, humbug.

Pee-Wee's big misadventure

'The other day I had an oddly Proustian little epiphany . . .' That, the opening phrase of my piece on Baudrillard's *La Guerre du Golfe n'a pas eu lieu*, subsequently found its way into *Private Eye*'s Pseuds Corner. Quite right, too, I have to say, although what shames me in retrospect is less the obvious affectation of 'epiphany' (when what I meant could have been communicated quite satisfactorily by an unpretentious word like 'shiver' or 'frisson') than the intellectual laziness of 'Proustian', now so intolerably hackneyed a qualifier for any experience connected with memory that it would merit inclusion in an updated edition of Flaubert's *Dictionnaire des idées reçues*.

Mea culpa, then. But, if I mention it here, it's not out of some almost unheard-of spasm of journalistic self-flagellation but because I consciously intend to offer *Private Eye* a specimen of which it can really make a meal. To wit: By far the most significant cultural event of the last few weeks, more significant than the appearance of the new Julian Barnes novel or the new Woody Allen film, more significant even than the 'Pizzarotti on the Park' concert, has been the downfall of Pee-Wee Herman.

For anyone unfamiliar with both the name and the story behind it, Pee-Wee Herman (alias Paul Reubens or Paul Rubenfeld) was throughout the eighties a cult performer on children's television in the United States; he also starred in two films, the first of which, *Pee-Wee's Big Adventure*, directed by Tim Burton, was by no means negligible. His extraordinarily fey persona, dapper, androgynous and terminally infantile, was directly descended not only from the great mimes of Hollywood silent slapstick, from Chaplin, Keaton, Harry Langdon and Fatty Arbuckle (whose disgrace prefigured his own), and in the era of the talkies from Harpo Marx and Jerry Lewis, but also and perhaps above all from such animated creations as Bugs Bunny, Daffy Duck and Woody Woodpecker. And what happened to this living cartoon was that he was arrested in a porn cinema in Florida on a charge of indecent exposure or, as the arresting officer chose to put it, 'manipulating the genitalia'.

His career, possibly his public life, is over. The television station CBS instantly cancelled repeats of his long-running show; Lionel Leisure, a prominent chain of toy stores, ordered its managers to remove all Pee-Wee-related items from their displays; a Japanese brokerage firm declined to renew a contract for a series of commercials; etc., etc.

It's an old, well-worn tale. An artist (which Reubens was) ascends a ladder and imagines that he has 'arrived'. He forgets that this is merely the prelude to his act, which consists of walking the tightrope above a crowd that has come to watch him break his neck. Reubens has just plummeted spectacularly from that tightrope.

There is, strangely, no more acute humiliation than to be caught doing in public what everyone does in private: farting, spitting, nose-picking, masturbating or otherwise assuaging one's bodily tensions. But although comedy has traditionally sublimated these activities (all squeaky noises off are basically metaphors of farting; all slapstick custard pies are bowdlerised substitutes for excrement – are what one might call *white shit*), and although children in particular are notorious for delighting in the multiple comico-erotic opportunities presented by the body's various orifices, there can be no salvation in society's eyes for a children's (and child-like) comic icon who actually reveals that he has genitalia to manipulate.

To be sure, Reubens (Pee-Wee Herman is dead) wilfully entered into this regressive, repressive covenant with society, he wilfully aligned himself with all the cute anthropomorphic hybrids of popular culture – the wise-cracking rabbits and the irascible ducks and the rosy-cheeked lead soldiers who whirr into life as soon as the bespectacled old toymaker has dozed off beside a glowing cartoon fire – the precise parameters of whose physical realism tend to raise troubling questions in the infant mind without ever daring to answer them. Was Rupert Bear the product of an immaculate conception or did his placid, pipe-smoking father really *do that thing* to his mother? Did she give birth to baby Rupert as a bear would or as the woman she was in anthropomorphic terms? Why does Donald Duck sport a jacket but go bottomless? Why does Mickey Mouse sound like a castrato? How come his behavioural patterns are those of a human being whereas Pluto's – Pluto, who was always much more resistant to anthropomorphism – obstinately remain those of a dog? A mouse with a dog for a pet? Why, just visible beyond the preppy white socks and sneakers of the eternal adolescent he seemed to be, did the sight of Jerry Lewis's bronzed and hairy legs disturb one so? And why did Pee-Wee Herman's neatly tapering little-boy's-first-grown-up-pair-of-trousers have flies, if not, for one reason or another, to enable him to pull out his penis? That, after all, is what trouser flies are for.

Had Reubens not been arrested for indecent exposure (and for his fans it was a double exposure, so to speak, since until the publication of his mug shots none of them had ever seen his true, unmade-up features), the last of these questions would have been left, like all the others, in a state of hypocritical and half-conscious suspension. His mistake was to have answered it.

Anthropomorphism consists less in transforming animals (whether real or animated) into human beings than in denying them their animality, their physicality. Even if, in the case of Pee-Wee Herman, the customary process was reversed – he strove to turn himself into a cartoon – what brought about his fall was also in its way a form of anthropomorphism, an unacceptably literal form. He showed that he was human. He exposed himself.

An en and one nought

There is a short story by Raymond Carver which has a lovely title: *What We Talk About When We Talk About Love*. What I especially appreciate about that title is its fastidious precision as a formula for interrogating the world: not 'What is . . .?' but 'What is it that we talk about when asking "What is . . .?"?' Exactly what is it, for example, that we talk about when we talk about Peter Greenaway?

According to the *Observer*, which recently published a 20-point 'bluffer's guide' to the director, we talk about 'colour-coded imagery, number-counting, misanthropy, nudity, obesity, obscurity, unhealthy interest in bodily functions, cannibalism, Michael Nyman music'. *Voilà*. Greenaway in a nutshell. (The newspaper in question clearly imagines that a line of ironic demarcation separates such a feature from ostensibly similar ones in the tabloids, dealing rather with Madonna, 'Gazza' and the Princess of Wales, but one has to say that in this instance its philistinism and incompetent fact-checking made it virtually indistinguishable from them.)

If most reviewers of *Prospero's Books* felt obliged to probe a little deeper than that, they too availed themselves, even when guardedly reticent about the film's ultimate value, of a cornucopious kitty of received opinions about Greenaway – opinions which, uniquely, *they received from the director himself.* Over the years, from *The Draughtsman's Contract* and *A Zed and Two Noughts* to *The Belly of an Architect* and *Drowning By Numbers*, the director has succeeded, with the (not necessarily conscious) intellectual terrorism of the polymath, in imposing the grid of his own subjective discourse on almost every objective attempt to discuss his films. Such is their exhaustive referentiality (to art history, biology, numerology, etc.) that one tends to write about them the way he talks about them or not write about them at all.

Hence, this time around, every critic duly cited the art-historical allusions which dot the film and for the most part attributed to them precisely the significance that Greenaway himself has done. Yet, if one were willing to risk approaching *Prospero's Books* from a less clammily orthodox angle, one might also compare such a strategy to the canny casting of big stars in cameo parts exploited by a film like *A Bridge Too Far.* Instead of squealing, 'Look, there's Robert Mitchum!' and 'Isn't that Michael Caine?', one finds oneself knowingly murmuring, 'Look, there's a Bellini' and 'Isn't that a Veronese?' There was, too, the dutiful and by now canonic reference to Alain Resnais and the mesmerically virtuoso tracking shots of *L'Année dernière à Marienbad*, the single filmmaker and film most frequently cited by Greenaway as having been an influence on his own work. Yet Resnais's tracking shots are frontal and exploratory, tirelessly redefining and reinventing the film's spatial parameters, whereas Greenaway's are almost always lateral and even somewhat treadmill-like, respectful of a purely theatrical and scenographic conception of space. Finally, there seemed to be a virtual consensus that the film, whatever might have been its incidental flaws, was a banquet for the senses, a positively Lucullan feast for the eyes. Yet here again, alas, it could be argued – rather, it could have been but wasn't argued – that, to mention only the most flagrant case, the décor of Caliban's grotto resembled nothing so much as one of Hamley's kitschier window displays on Christmas Eve.

Actually, I take no pleasure in being disobliging about Greenaway. Although always with real reservations, I would count myself among his admirers (in particular, *The Cook, the Thief, His Wife and Her Lover* struck me as a magnificently slimy allegory of the Thatcherite eighties) and for the man himself I have a high regard. Yet I found *Prospero's Books* not simply a disheartening experience, such as might be the case with the failure of any artist one esteems, but a perplexingly *detestable* one – perplexing, that is, until I myself managed at last to crawl out from beneath the thicket of his preprogrammed discourse and began to understand that my reaction was related to the fact that practically everyone in the film is naked.

Greenaway's rehabilitation of the nude, a predominant iconographic theme of Western art history and, at least until fairly recently, a notable absentee from the history of the cinema, is yet another crucial key to his sensibility which he has personally presented to his exegetes. But although nudes have been increasingly elbowing clothed performers out of his films, an evolution attaining its delirious apogee with the hundred-odd stark naked extras of *A TV Dante* and *Prospero's Books*, and although Greenaway himself has often spoken of the greater affinity he has always felt with painters than with his fellow filmmakers, no direct equation should ever be established between painting a nude and filming a nude. There is a realism and a transparency proper to the filmic image which defies comparison with the distancing and decorporifying effect of paint and canvas, and a film studio wholly lacks the insulating privacy of a painter's studio. A film director, in short, has a very real responsibility towards those of his performers who agree to take their clothes off for him, the responsibility never to degrade or humiliate them.

Yet the glum nudes I saw paraded in *Prospero's Books* were those not of art history but rather of the anatomy treatise, the dissecting table and the morgue. That in itself, perhaps, is legitimate, a way like any other of looking at the naked human body. (It's extremely moving in Greenaway's beautiful short film *Death in the Seine*.) And it eventually dawned on me that what I found so disturbing was not their nudity but their numbers, those damned Greenawayesque numbers. In the cinema, and I hold this to be almost axiomatic, *there should never be more than two nude bodies in the same shot* (or possibly, in exceptional circumstances, three). More than that – ten, let's say – and, no matter how unimpeachable the director's intentions might have been, the image becomes irrevocably pornographic, the pornography of the orgy. Still more – Greenaway's hundred-odd – and, even if only as the unwitting reflection of a collective memory, the concentration camps are not far away.

Terminators

However unpalatable the experience, it is important that from time to time we read the great pessimists. Adorno, for example, Theodor W. Adorno, one of the quadrangular pillars of the Frankfurt School of 'critical theory' (alongside Herbert Marcuse, Walter Benjamin and Max Horkheimer), a philosopher, sociologist, critic and, if not quite as thoroughgoing a naysayer as Cioran or Thomas Bernhard, an indefatigable scourge of the barbarism of mass culture and a man whose nightmarish stringency, even rigidity, of intellect has made him now completely unfashionable.

Oh, but he was a terror, Adorno! Only he could have written, in an essay on Bach published in the postwar collection *Prisms*, that, by comparison with the 'infinitely involuted' transcendence of the master of Leipzig, 'Mozart's proverbial grace is, as pure musical *peinture*, rather crass and mechanical'; or that, upon returning to Beethoven after a 'prolonged, intensive study of Bach', he felt 'as though he were confronted by a kind of decorative light music, which only the culture-cliché could consider "profound"'. Mozart *crass*? Beethoven *light*? How would the jazz-abhorring Adorno react, one wonders, if confronted by fans of musical comedy who speak of Stephen Sondheim as though he were the combination and distillation of both?

What one cannot help wondering, indeed, is how a thinker like Adorno would fare in this postmodern world of ours, a world in which a time-honoured process of cultural assimilation has been neatly reversed – where once the intellectually respectable would eventually filter down to the popular imagination, it's now the products of that popular imagination which are at permanent risk of becoming intellectually respectable. It's a trend that has been steadily evolving throughout the eighties and early nineties, so that it should not surprise us that, officialising it with the clinching seal of intellectual approval, a magazine entirely devoted to populist culture is about to be launched. (Magazines, not books, are the repository of the postmodern zeitgeist.) The *Modern Review* is financed by Julie Burchill, doubtless impatient to pay her dues to the culture which has made her wealthy; a typical article in its dummy presentation issue is a laudatory review of *The Silence of the Lambs* – Thomas Harris's novel, not the recent film version – by Professor Eric Griffiths; and, needless to say, all the usual suspects have been rounded up to contribute to it (including yours truly – but just as every man has his price, so every man must somewhere draw a line, and I draw mine at Julie Burchill).

Actually, it was reading the *Modern Review*'s 'manifesto' (which, bizarrely, alludes to the Frankfurt School), and reading more or less concurrently the rave reviews received from practically every quarter by James Cameron's *Terminator II*, that even I, who have written on popular culture for some years now, began to feel that enough was enough.

For when I see a film like *Terminator II* I tend to have recourse to a phrase beloved of my late grandmother: 'Grown men!' I realise that these grown men, most notably the film's director and star, earned millions of dollars apiece to make it, whereas I, to write this article condemning it, will earn – well, never mind, but less. I realise, too, that the film's narrative is 'brilliantly paced', that its action 'never lets up' and that its special effects are stupendous (my problem with special effects is that I rather enjoy them but loathe the films in which they are deployed) – I nevertheless cannot help thinking 'Grown men!'

This, surely, is quite the stupidest cinema in the world, the Coca-Cola, the McDonald's of the cinema – the cinema of arrested development. In *Terminator II* the concept of filmic spectacle is indissolubly linked, as though by definition, with the most extreme, most cretinous forms of violence and havoc, with what the critic André Bazin once termed the filmgoer's chronic 'Nero complex' – the vicarious delight that one may find oneself all too insidiously taking in wholescale devastation.

Its stupidity, moreover, resides not only in its general barbarity of texture and tone but also in its narrative detail. Consider one example: Arnold Schwarzenegger, the good terminator, is so comprehensively programmed in earth-lore that, in order to outsmart his arch-enemy, the evil terminator, he contrives to conjure out of his software the name 'Wolfie' as being a reasonable one for a child's pet dog. (It's an old trick of interrogators: the dog's real name is Max, but because the evil terminator fails to query 'Wolfie' his cover is blown.) Yet later, when some turn of the plot gives his teenage protegé, the dog's master, cause to weep, Schwarzenegger stares at him blankly and asks, 'What's the matter with your eyes?' Thus we are asked to believe that his devisers would programme him with the name 'Wolfie' but forget to programme the not exactly negligible datum that when human beings are distressed their eyes shed tears. Did no reviewer notice this? Or were they too dazzled by the film's special effects to attend to its special defects?

Perhaps most dispiriting, however, is the revelation that *Termi-*

nator II's projected 'future' is the same weary old postnuclear apocalypse familiar to us from scores of pulpy science-fiction novels and films, a reassuringly conventionalised future in which embattled resistants gamely debate the radioactive rubble with marauding robots, an amazingly *dated* future whose principal signifier is that trusty Vernian prop, the automatically sliding door. Whereas, as Adorno knew, a very much more legitimate fear of the future is that it will merely be the continuation and intensification of the present, with even more Coca-Colas, even more McDonalds and even more *Terminators*.

It was another of the great pessimists, Elias Canetti, who once remarked that he could no longer look at a map of the world without having his nostrils fill with the smell of burning flesh. These days, when I look at a map of the world, my nostrils are filled with something almost as putrid – the stench of millions of Big Macs and Big Arnies.

The Tardis doctrine

One of the first of many disappointments in the life of the Narrator of Proust's *Recherche* is his seriocomic encounter, at Mme Swann's dinner table, with an idol of his adolescence, the writer Bergotte. As he notes with no little dismay, Bergotte, the *précieux*, the ineffably subtle stylist, invariably confines himself, when discoursing on literature, to citing, and in the most insipidly uncommunicative terms at that, remembered passages from books which he has particularly admired. 'Ah yes, it's very fine!' he will remark of a scene in some fashionable novel. 'There's a little girl in an orange shawl!'

Bergotte's fastidious distaste for abstractions on any level is really quite typical of nineteenth-century literary and art criticism, whose primary characteristic, from our own theory-crazy vantage point, is its bizarre shortage of ideas. Whereas, nowadays, most self-respecting critics feel obligated to guarantee their editors and readers practically an idea per sentence, even Baudelaire, even Ruskin, among the very greatest of the last century's art critics, used up a now inadmissible amount of space on detailed descriptions of subject-matter. So leisurely, so literal-minded, an attitude to exegesis may cause the contemporary reader to chafe at the bit sometimes. Yet there are times, too, when one finds oneself confronted with a work of art for which the analytical approach remains stubbornly inadequate and may even prove to be counter-productive.

Such a work, as far as I'm concerned, is Akira Kurosawa's new film *Rhapsody in August*, derided by almost every reviewer in this country as an embarrassingly naïve, schematic, didactic and tendentiously partial anti-nuclear tract. All of which it is, I suppose – yet it is also, in my solitary opinion, an absolute, half Griffithian, half Rossellinian, masterpiece. I find myself incapable, though, of conveying exactly why I think so, except by description.

Let me focus, like Bergotte, on a single detail. In one early sequence of the film four youthful, Americanised, gum-chewing siblings are being served a meal by their aged, traditionalist, kimono-clad grandmother in the latter's wood-and-paper house. To Western eyes the tiny, bent grandmother is a living Hokusai print and her exquisite-looking fare is laid out with the proper symmetrical daintiness. Exquisite it looks and exquisite it must taste: that is a given of such a situation in such a film. Imagine the Western spectator's astonishment, then, when, after a good deal of furtive whispering, one of the children finally dares to inform his poor grandmother that her food is revolting, gooily inedible pap!

Now, it should first be pointed out that here too a didactic intention can perhaps be inferred, it being not entirely evident (for non-Japanese audiences) whether the meal in question is objectively inedible or whether the children's palates have been corrupted by hamburgers and Cokes. Whichever it is, the uncomprehending old dear stares at them for a few agonising instants and slowly bows her head. And then? That's it: she slowly bows her head, it's very fine! But, you ask, what about it? I repeat: That's all there is to it, it's just the way she bows her head, it's a stroke of genius, it's very fine, I was moved to tears, what more do you want? Analysis or at the very least an idea. Sorry. She bows her head, it's indefinably beautiful, she's a great actress, Kurosawa is a great director of actors. She bows her head.

Ideally, I would prefer to leave things at that. If I had to generalise, however, I would call this (after *Doctor Who*) the Tardis doctrine of criticism: within a single detail, a detail as humble and as measurable as a telephone booth, there may be contained a whole world. For another example, take Tim Albery's superb production of Britten's *Billy Budd* at the London Coliseum. The opera (so absorbing it produces a strange variant on the suspension of disbelief: *one forgets that it is being sung*) is narrated by the elderly, now retired Captain Vere, former master of the *Indomitable* aboard which Billy was hanged from the yardarm for having fatally struck a superior officer, the sadistic Claggart. Forlornly hovering on the edge of the production's quasi-abstract décor, still haunted by his perhaps cowardly failure to save the handsome, innocent lad from his undeserved fate, Vere at one point wanders over to a railing from which he gazes down into an unspecified void.

This railing is a modest prop, which one at first assumes was added to the set simply to give Vere something to lean on. Then one gradually comes to realise that it is precisely the sort of railing that one would expect to find along the promenade of a South Coast resort like Bournemouth or Eastbourne; that such a resort is precisely the sort of spot a lonely, unmarried old sea-captain would retire to; that he is gazing down at the sea to which, for better or worse, he devoted the greater part of his life; and that, who knows, he may even be contemplating suicide.

So much contained in so little: it is, in short, the paradigmatic miracle of art, the miracle of the loaves and fishes.

P. S. Finding myself with space to spare, I should like to make use of it to demonstrate just how the delirious idea-spinning I mention above can lead one (or, rather, me) into intemperate glibness. Recently, writing of *Prospero's Books*, I took it upon myself to compare its images of nudity with the collective documented memory of the concentration camps. The oh-so-clever crassness and stupidity of that oh-so-clever analogy have been the cause of my lying awake at night, of my suddenly, and more than once, blushing in the street. Without prompting from anyone, then, I now wish unreservedly to withdraw it and apologise to Peter Greenaway. I bow my head.

The theatre and its backlist

I have always, perhaps not quite rationally, believed in the power of names to influence the destinies of those who bear them. I believe, specifically, that as with many a marriage of convenience (which is, when one thinks of it, a fair description of being yoked for ever to a name that was not of one's own choice) one grows increasingly close to one's name, gradually identifying with it, either striving to live up to it or struggling to live it down. I believe, finally, that in the hierarchy of artistic and intellectual achievement a name may often serve as a guide to the current status of a reputation; that one frivolous but uncannily reliable method of measuring fame is to assess whether a celebrity's surname is weighty enough, has sufficient éclat, to face the scrutiny of the world on its own.

Take the contemporary English theatre. We say 'Pinter', naturally, just 'Pinter'. (The dramatist's name has in fact advanced to a subsequent stage in the process where, under 'Pinteresque', it has entered the language.) We say, if in this case a little bit less securely, 'Stoppard'. And we say 'Ayckbourn', although that name does ring a trifle tinnily all by itself: if it occurred to us to mention it in the same breath as that of Congreve or Sheridan, we would probably feel compelled after all to add the 'Alan'. (Thus: 'Three famous writers of English comedies-of-manners are Congreve, Sheridan and *Alan* Ayckbourn.') But who, other than a professional critic in the context of a review, would ever feel at ease referring just to 'Hare'? Or 'Brenton'? Or 'Barker'? The temptation, the internal, almost instinctive pressure, to complete the name, to refer instead to '*David* Hare', to '*Howard* Brenton' and to '*Howard* Barker' is all but irresistible. Not that I am proposing this little game as representing any kind of serious critical methodology; but it is a useful shorthand for evaluating an artist's standing at a given moment in his or her career.

The other day I happened to note a name on the poster for a forthcoming revival of *Becket* at the Haymarket Theatre – that of the play's author, Jean Anouilh. Or, rather, 'Anouilh'. 'Anooeeh.' Such a queer, lip-puckeringly unpronounceable name, yet one which, even now, when very few of Anouilh's plays are ever performed, remains conjurable enough.

Why so? In the sixties, when scarcely a year passed without some starrily prestigious production of one of his works – one might cite, in chronological disorder, *Poor Bitos* with Donald Pleasance, *The Waltz of the Toreadors* with Leo McKern, *The Fighting Cock* with John Clements, *The Rehearsal* with Phyllis Calvert and Maggie Smith, *Dear Antoine* with Edith Evans and Clements again – Anouilh was widely regarded as belonging to a still vital tradition encompassing the sparkling verbal preciosity of Cocteau and Giraudoux, the weary, *gemütlich* cynicism of Molnar and Schnitzler, and the radical exploration of theatrical illusionism that continues to bear the name of its pioneering spirit, Pirandello.

By the mid-seventies, however, his work had come to seem both reactionary and repetitive, trotting out as it regularly did that old vaudeville duo, Appearance and Reality, for yet another benefit performance, like Neil Simon's Sunshine Boys. In Paris, which is where I lived during the decade, it would have been quite unthinkable for one to go see, let alone confess to admiring, an Anouilh play. And nothing since, I have to say, had ever caused me to revise the view I formed of him then, as a jaundiced, misanthropic has-been, ripe for the brimming dustbins of theatrical history.

Well, I was wrong. Reading or re-reading these plays, what I have discovered is a neoclassicism which has become suddenly, pristinely, classic, a neoromanticism that is as perverse as it is fey. I have discovered, too, or rather rediscovered, his matchless stagecraft. In Anouilh's plays, no matter their setting or subject-matter, *the theatre shows through*. Like Pirandello, he never forgot that the word 'theatre' applies not merely to an art form but to the place in which it is celebrated.

But, precisely, that wizardry of stagecraft, that celebration of the theatre for its own sake – what has happened to it? These days it's practically unheard-of for a new play staged in London to aspire much higher than to a kind of theatricalised journalism. The dramatist appropriates a theme from the headlines, stuffs it with knowing and instantly identifiable references, whips the odd allegorical curlicue once around the blender – and, hey presto, a 'topical' drama with, if it's lucky, a shelf-life of six months. In the course of an *Observer* review, Michael Coveney listed such apparently crucial elements of Timberlake Wertenbaker's new play about the art world, *Three birds alighting on a field*, as a 'Home Counties Sloaney', Benenden, *Brookside*, the Channel 4 News, White's Club, Philip Glass, 'Schnabelisation', the political situation in Romania, NHS queues, Turks coerced into selling off their kidneys to Harley Street surgeons, 'a Muriel Gray-type critic', Kenwood and 'a magazine called "Elan"'. In thirty years' time, were the play to be revived, who would make sense of all that?

The answer, of course, is that it won't be revived, just as virtually no plays from the sixties, when this journalistic mentality first became prevalent, are revived or revivable today – not one of those quixotically fearless and violent exposés of Poulson and Rachman and the like that were systematically acclaimed by the critics of the time as recharging the batteries of the British theatre. Yet, if it is to survive, the theatre, like a publishing house, needs a *backlist*. It needs journalists, yes, but it has a far greater need of poets. (Anouilh himself, for that matter, was never exclusively the confectioner of theatrical marzipan that his current reputation would suggest. His *Antigone* had for its first audiences in the forties an unmissable relevance to the embattled realities of Occupied Paris.) Above all, it needs worthy and enduring surnames. Otherwise it will be the fate of every new play – as is said, precisely, of every newspaper – to find itself wrapping up yesterday's fish and chips.

The seven myths of homosexuality

There is in the word 'heterosexuality' a paradox: whenever one sees it in print, one thinks immediately of homosexuals. Such a diametric transference of meaning will be interpreted by some as a symptom of the increasing entrenchment of sexual deviance; in reality, what it implies is the exact reverse. In a society like ours, however enlightened it flatters itself to be, it is precisely because heterosexuality is still an oppressive cultural 'norm' that any writer electing to treat it as an option instead of as a destiny (the sort of writer who would describe Wagner's *Tristan and Isolde*, say, as an exaltation of specifically *heterosexual*, and not merely sexual, passion) is making a distinction still so very uncommon that its effect is to remind one above all of the deviations from that norm.

There is, in addition, the fact that homosexuals define themselves – are, as an alienated minority, etymologically coerced into defining themselves – in sexual rather than social, professional or familial terms. So that anyone candidly, publicly, assuming a homosexual identity must also be prepared to assume the inference likely to be drawn that he (or she: but my concern here is with male homosexuality) is primarily a sexual being, someone for whom sex is particularly, even excessively important. Possibly still more than the practices which define his sexuality, it is the liberated homosexual's candour that makes him such a threatening and subversive figure.

Much the same applies to homosexuality in the arts – a novel or film or play about homosexuals is usually judged on the basis of its subject-matter alone – and that is where the problem arises. The subject is not inexhaustible. Or, rather, it *is* inexhaustible, but it has to be constantly reinvented, replenished with new themes, new myths, new iconographies and new frames of reference. I find gay art nowadays increasingly circular, incestuous and self-referential (I expect, of course, to be bombarded with counter-examples); and to while away the time that I wasted during Todd Haynes's award-laden but amateurishly inept film *Poison*, I amused myself by cataloguing what I see as seven elemental homosexual mythologies (like those seven basic plotlines in one or several of which it is claimed every fictional narrative is anchored), all of which strike me as having already said everything of value that they ever had to say.

1. The Genet mythology of the muscly, tattooed thief and convict, his shaven head garlanded with pink roses, his trousers concealing what might be termed, with an appropriately delicate indelicacy, an *anus mirabilis*. This is a mythology which, generally divested of its existentialist properties, has informed some of William Burroughs's novels, the films of Pasolini, Fassbinder and Kenneth Anger (as well as *Poison*) and a lot of junky pornography, and its reductive signifier is (in the visual arts) the *bulge*.

2. Genet, however, was also a (self-confessed) thief in his writings, much of his personal mythology having been filched from

Cocteau, whose *louche* sailors, convicts, cyclists, angels and glaziers were more demurely graceful and teasing than any of his disciple's rough trade – except in some erotic line drawings of startling explicitness. (The latter clearly had a strong influence on Hockney, whose line-drawing illustrations to Cavafy's poems constitute perhaps the most accurate and legitimate *translation* of the Greek poet.)

3. A not entirely dissimilar vein is that associated in this country with the work of Derek Jarman, in whose films homosexuality or queerness, as he prefers to call it, has been mythologised as one long, glum, narcissistic martyrology (as present in Thatcher's Britain as, courtesy of Wilfred Owen, on Flanders Field). The patron saint of this martyrology is unquestionably Sebastian, although he has been upstaged of late by Christ, whose prestige as a martyr is enhanced by His historical radicalism vis-à-vis an authoritarian State, by the inherent pathos of religious mysticism and by His own grace under pressure, literally, on the Cross.

4. In a film like Ron Peck's *Nighthawks*, by contrast, as equally in several stage and television dramas, it is the more problematic aspects of homosexuality which have predominated, with gay men portrayed as 'creatures of the shadows', terrified of exposure and trapped in an endless, joyless treadmill trawl from pub to club. This is a salutary and easily denigrated form of cinéreportage but, if given half a chance (which Peck has certainly given it), its 'realism' will fatally descend into outright miserabilism.

5. From the United States, from Gore Vidal (in *The City and the Pillar*) and more recently Edmund White (in *A Boy's Own Story*), there has come to us what might be thought of as the 'Summer of 69' approach, in which is evoked the moment of trembling self-discovery, the ritual passage of confused and tormented adolescence into uncomplexed homosexual manhood – as inevitably affecting as is any account of a sentimental education but now, surely, stale from repetition.

6. It is still a good deal more affecting than the maudlin, self-

pitying, show-business homosexual – wisecracking through his tears the way the heroines of Victorian melodramas used to smile through theirs – personified most nauseatingly by Harvey Fierstein in both the original Broadway stage and subsequent Hollywood film version of his own *Torch Song Trilogy*, a play that is not so much mawk*ish* as downright *mawk*. Considering, after all, that in the course of its three acts his protagonist is privileged to enjoy a fulfilling relationship with, respectively (if hardly respectably), a hunky married man, an exquisitely personable lover in his early twenties and a surrogate teenage son, precisely what is he to be pitied for?

7. There is, finally, perhaps the oldest of all overtly gay mythologies, descended from Wilde, Firbank and Coward: homosexuality as a repository of wit, elegance and fantasy. (It still exists.)

In its constructive, creative phase each (or almost each) of these mythologies produced a rich and various seam of meaning, and the culture of the twentieth century would have been diminished without it. Yet they all represent ideas whose time has come and gone, and one would like to think of them as belonging rather to the prehistory of a period of writing and thinking and dreaming about homosexuality as, simply, the most natural thing in the world. Well, yes, all right, the second most natural.

Andy Warhol

The critics are right: the Pop Art retrospective at the Royal Academy is a calamity. With a very few exceptions, the exhibits are the most awful, artless trumpery, many of them, indeed, out-and-out eyesores. And the experience is particularly dispiriting for someone who happens to be old enough, as I myself am, to remember the movement *from the first time around* and whose memory of its most characteristic products was one of wit, flair, exuberance and enviably inexhaustible charm. That memory has now gone, unlikely ever to be revived; and the principal service rendered by the exhibition is that it forces one yet again to stub one's eyes, so to speak, on the work of a real and enduring enigma: Andy Warhol.

As it happens, I have been belatedly reading his *Diaries*, whose entry for January 26, 1986, alluding to the sale of a table for $1.2 million at Sotheby's in New York, concludes with this sardonic aside: 'Now what people want is only one of a kind. My art is just the opposite.'

Poor Warhol! Here he is, belatedly confronted with the paradox (or one of the numerous paradoxes) of his public persona, his professional identity: by producing works that were deliberately not 'one of a kind', that is what he became. The more systematically he *cloned* his imagery, indefatigably replicating his Maos, Marilyns and Jackies, the more inimitable, irreproducible and irreplaceable he himself appeared. So influential was the mystique of mass-production on his conception of art (and its terrible twin, finance) that he actually went as far as to advertise as a portraitist in Nieman-Marcus's Christmas gift catalogue of 1986, a depth of self-prostitution at which even some of his hangers-on balked. And if he could only have extended the process to its logical conclusion, its absurdist point of no return – matching every single soup can to roll off the Campbell production line with its very own numbered painting or print from the production line of his (unironically named) Factory – then he might indeed have been, as the film critic Michael O'Pray recklessly described him in the introduction to a recent season of his films at the NFT, 'perhaps the most famous artist of the 20th century'.

Such was Warhol's originality; and, in a neophiliac world like ours, originality is what makes art both tick and pay. Why, even his cynicism started to seem innovatory. Great art (one can almost hear him saying to himself) is art that is widely reproduced; therefore, reversing the axiom, art that is widely reproduced will necessarily be perceived as great. And, terrified that posterity would decline to undertake the task for him, or else unwilling to wait that long, he coolly set about reproducing his work within his and its own lifetime.

It is perhaps worth noting, though, that originality, even when it materialises in so overtly debased and mercenary a guise, continues nevertheless to retain something of its sting. Although Warhol scarcely died a penniless *artiste maudit*, none of his paintings has ever sold or is ever likely to sell for the sort of stratospheric seven-digit prices now quite routinely fetched by such contemporaries of his as Robert Rauschenberg and Jasper Johns. Critics and collectors may publicly laud the almost piratical swagger with which, via the mass-produced and, as it were, *anonymous* individuality of his portraiture, he obliged all of us to reconsider the traditional values, codes and practices of the art world, but they have proved noticeably more reticent when it comes to putting their money where their mouths are – which is probably as close to being truly *maudit* as any contemporary artist can hope to get.

At the very beginning of the introduction cited above, O'Pray poses a question that, blunt as it is, hovers naggingly over the posthumous Warhol oeuvre: 'Genius or charlatan?' Since there *are* charlatans around (not a few in Warhol's own retinue), such a question is still perfectly valid with reference to any artist for whom extravagant conceptualist claims have been made. Yet I cannot help wondering whether in this instance it hasn't been wrongly posed. One of the characteristics of Warhol's work was the brio with which it succeeded in dissolving a number of art-historical contradictions (the contradiction between painting and photography, between the unique and the ubiquitous, between high art and popular culture), and it may be to him, if to anyone, that the old, conventional distinction between genius and charlatanism need no longer be applied.

Think, precisely, of his most emblematic icon, the Campbell's Soup Can. Setting aside the factor of individual talent (or genius), the impact it makes upon us, whether in its reproduced or its 'original' state, is exactly comparable to that generated by the most replicated image in the world, the Mona Lisa. Each of these icons, through its very ubiquity and familiarity, has been dispossessed of the pathos and resonance, the potential for eternally renewed discovery and assessment, that we tend to regard as essential properties of any great work of art; each of them has become the impassive and transparent image of itself; and if it is by virtue of a faintly kitschy element of myth and mystery, the fabled enigma of the lady's smile, that the Mona Lisa currently enjoys such universal favour, it could actually be by another mystery – genius or charlatan? – that Warhol's paintings will be kept alive.

I would argue, in fact, that Andy Warhol was neither a genius nor a charlatan but something halfway between: a bluffer. A bluffer, I should add, in the legitimate and unpejorative sense in which the word is employed in the game of poker. For if the Mona Lisa's so-called 'enigmatic' smile is precisely that of a poker player in the act of bluffing (take a good look at her), then that selfsame smile is present in virtually all of Warhol's work, except that it's to be found on the artist's face rather than the model's.

D'Annunzio

A couple of weeks ago, when telephoning my publisher, I found myself connected with a secretary to whom my name clearly meant nothing. I patiently spelled it out for her. She sniggered. 'You aren't by any chance Red Adair, are you?' 'No,' I snapped back, 'I'm unread Adair.'

It was just a joke (I hope), but it did call to mind a writer whose initials I happen to share and whom one might reasonably suppose to be currently unread, save perhaps in his native country:

Gabriele d'Annunzio. D'Annunzio – he who once reigned almost unchallenged in the pantheon of literary notoriety as poet, novelist, dramatist and philosopher (of a kind); who lent his name to a fashionable, turn-of-the-century pseudo-Nietzschean 'ism' that would subsequently be poured into the ideological mix of Mussolinian Fascism; who was and to the end of his life remained irresistible, as they used to say, to women (in spite of his total baldness in later years and a dandified turkey-cock stockiness which made him look like a hard-boiled egg inside a Fabergé eggcup), the lover of, among many, many others, the actress Eleanora Duse and the eccentric socialite, the Marchesa Casati, whose freakishly white-skinned, anorexically thin torso and lipstick-slashed mouth made her, for her part, look like a thermometer in a cloche hat; he who in 1919 'liberated' and for sixteen months singlehandedly governed the northern Italian town of Fiume, previously occupied by the French; he who ultimately withdrew into his extraordinary house on Lake Garda, the Vittoriale, whose every room is a treasure vault, whose every mantelpiece is a masterpiece, and on whose walls, in the Maestro's own boudoir, hang 'the gloves forgotten by all those ladies who lost their heads' – d'Annunzio unread? How can that be?

In fact, it is not exactly so. In Britain there would appear to be at least the stirrings of a revival of interest in him, by virtue mainly of the efforts of a small and admirable publishing house named Dedalus, which operates out of a village near Cambridge and specialises in the Decadents. Aside from d'Annunzio (notably, *The Triumph of Death, The Child of Pleasure* and *The Victim*, all of them in glossily elegant paperbacks), it has reissued translations of such neglected masters of curdled *fin de siècle* prose as Octave Mirbeau, Gustav Meyrink, Leonid Andreyev and J.-K. Huysmans. In 1988 the Carcanet Press published a volume of d'Annunzio's verse, *Halcyon*, and Quartet is about to bring out *The Flame of Life*, a self-glorifying account of his affair with Duse.

It would be idle to suggest that d'Annunzio has not seriously dated or that his attitudinising heroes and enervated heroines have much to say that is of immediate and quantifiable 'relevance' to us. Yet the interest of his novels is far from exclusively historical. Put simply, they are, even in translation, far superior to virtually anything being written now in English. Who after all can write like this today (a description of the ocean, one such passage from among many, in *The Triumph of Death*)?

'Here and there a wandering breeze would lift and hurry the waves a little; their delicate crests curled – stole a gleam from the luminous sunset – foamed for an instant, and sank over languidly, now with a clash of cymbals, now like crystal balls rolling down an inclined plane. Fresh waves rose in their place engendered by an increase in the wind, curled over limpidly, carrying in their curve all the grace of the dying day, breaking with a gentle indolence like the swaying of white rose-bushes, and leaving patches of foam like petals on the glassy mirror of the sea.'

Why, then, should a writer like d'Annunzio, why should the deviser of prose so ornate, so fiendishly curlicued, yet also, after all, so accurately observed, be suffering his present neglect? The reason is, I think, threefold:

First, he has fallen victim to our current fixation on rehabilitating artists solely for their precursory 'modernity', artists, in other words, whose formal or thematic preoccupations prefigure those of our own era. In this respect, however, it might be worth reminding ourselves that our own specific 'modernity' will not last forever; that, precisely, its own formal and thematic preoccupations will yield to others whose outline we cannot as yet predict; and that the artists who foreshadowed it may not be to anything like the same degree compatible with the zeitgeist that succeeds it. The holy Kafka, for example: hard as it is to credit now, there will indeed come a time when his intuition of the modern world strikes us (or our descendants) as irrevocably passé.

Second, in strict preservationist terms, no art medium can be said to enjoy absolutely equal status with any other. Hence, while the republishing of a neglected writer may pose a lesser financial burden than the revival of a once popular, now seldom staged play, it is still a good deal costlier and riskier than buying up joblots of old movies for TV screenings – which is why film buffs are granted a more direct and extensive contact with the historical trivia of their chosen medium than is the case with specialists in any other field.

Finally, the crucial question of how 'posterity' functions has to be addressed. Even if most of us tend to regard posterity as a form of natural selection, authentically Darwinian in the mercilessness with which it winnows out all but the fittest for survival, it remains, when all is said and done, a human operation contingent upon human taste and prejudice and all too likely to be compromised by human error. Its kinship, therefore, is rather with the fallible and occasionally quite arbitrary jury system, except that, instead of twelve good men and true, it is by thousands of critics and historians that works of art are acquitted or condemned. Experts all of them, I dare say, but who would risk claiming that there has never been a miscarriage of justice?

Illusions of grandeur

I recall, when I recently saw *Crimes and Misdemeanors*, remarking to an acquaintance that what was beginning to irritate me about Woody Allen was the insidious manner in which, over the last decade, his cinematic persona had undergone an apparently irreversible conversion from the neurotic schlemiel of such earlier films as *Annie Hall, Broadway Danny Rose* and *Zelig* (the best, in my opinion) to the almost saintly repository of truth and wisdom which has since become the image he is concerned to project of himself. When my acquaintance protested that something of the schlemiel could nevertheless be said to remain in *Crimes and Misdemeanors*, in view of the fact that, by the end of the film, Allen's character is chagrined to find Mia Farrow snatched from him by his rival, a smarmily urbane television producer played by Alan Alda, I thought it worth pointing out that, for his public, Allen does in fact *get* Mia Farrow – offscreen if not on. For, after all, we know that Farrow and he are married and he knows that we know and we know that he knows that we know.

The point, I believe, is not at all a trivial one, since it seems to contradict the fundamental principle of cinematic illusionism, that immemorial process of mystification and often manipulation whereby we are willingly inveigled into forgetting that what we are watching is a mere imitation of life and (if for no longer than the film's duration) contentedly delude ourselves that it is all the real thing, shedding genuine tears, for example, at the spectacle of famous, highly paid superstars, people obscenely better off than we are, pretending to suffer.

That we do so is evidently a tribute to their own gifts as actors and actresses. But only in part: for I would suggest that what causes our tears to gush as generously as they do is also our knowledge that these suffering individuals up there on the screen *know that they are being watched*. They know (which is to say, the actors and actresses know, but this knowledge cannot help but subtly influence the way in which they fashion their characters) that they are not suffering alone – even if, in the context of the film's narrative, they *are* suffering alone. In fact, these sufferings, these acts of supposedly discreet self-abnegation and heroically inconspicuous altruism, are being played out in front of rows and rows of sniffling spectators.

What a fantasy! Who could not be saintly under those conditions? Who could not do as cocky James Cagney does, in the marvellous old Warner Bros gangster movie *Angels With Dirty Faces* – pretend to be dragged kicking and screaming to the electric chair in order to turn a band of street kids, whose adulated role model he had been, from a life of crime (a scene that haunted me when I first saw the film in my adolescence) – if it were guaranteed that millions of spectators would be observing and appreciating the sacrifice? That, perhaps, is the true seduction of illusionism, that is what we all truly respond to – the impossibility, an impossibility proper to fiction in its every form, of *anonymity*.

Yet there does exist in 'real life' a category of individuals who enjoy an exactly similar privilege to that of fictional characters: celebrities. Think of it. You have been quietly and privately sending off cheques to aid famine victims in Africa? Why, your reward will be in Heaven. Bob Geldof, on the other hand, raises funds for the same cause and rumours of the Nobel Peace Prize start to circulate. You have been labouring unsung for thirty years over your first novel? Don't call us, we'll call you. Harold Brodkey labours for thirty years over his first novel and contrives to hype those labours, to *hype his silence* (which must be some kind of a first for the literary classes), to a foaming fever pitch in two continents? You make the discovery one fine day that you are HIV-positive? Then you may well encounter that pseudo-sanitary isolation, that unspoken quarantine, that ApartheAids, that still exists in spite of the eerie calm which seems to have settled upon the whole question. Derek Jarman is diagnosed HIV-positive and his chipper, plucky stoicism only enhances the respect in which he is already held.

My intention in citing these examples is certainly not to denigrate celebrities as such, for they too are destined to suffer in this vale of tears and may be just as saintly and altruistic as the next man. Nor is the living out of one's life in public without its own drawbacks. (One need only remind oneself of what happened to Nancy Reagan.) But the analogy I have drawn between the famous and the fictional should serve at the very least as a useful reminder of just how much there is separating those who star in the great movie of the world from the rest of us who will ever have to be content with merely gawping at the screen.

Variations on a theme park

Since it is this year that the very first European Disneyworld, situated not far from Paris, is finally scheduled to open to the public, the question that a number of my Parisian acquaintances have been asking for some little while is: Exactly what public? For their pardonably snobbish fear, I have to say, is that the *ville-lumière* risks becoming – notably, for the type of yobocratic British tourist that, to the French's good fortune, has traditionally preferred the homelier temptations of the Costa Brava – the 'gateway' to the new theme park.

A more refined Orlando, perhaps. Orlando is the city in Florida at which alight visitors to the ever-expanding complex of theme parks – Disney's The Magic Kingdom and EPCOT, SeaWorld, MGM and Universal – located in its environs. The city itself no doubt thrives as an autonomous residential and commercial community, but, having just returned from a visit to the parks, and still finding myself dusting pixilated dandruff from my shoulders, I'm reminded of Gertrude Stein's laconic judgment on Oakland: 'There's no there there.' Orlando appears to exist exclusively to lend a name to its airport; that at least is all Disney's pilgrims are likely to see of it, since the parks themselves sprawl so exorbitantly that there are times one despairs of ever again rejoining the outside world.

Dimension, in fact, is a crucial parameter of the theme park experience. Because, once inside, one gradually starts to forfeit all sense of what the outside was like, the theme park ends, in one's mind, by coinciding with the world itself, of which it becomes a hyperreal, homogenised and hygienically purified simulacrum, an all-enfolding experiment in virtual reality. And if one does somehow succeed in quitting one of the parks, the punctuation of highway signs inexorably propels one on to another, and another, and then another. The very landscape one traverses, green, glittering and even, is a theme park of sorts: nature as God's golf course.

Within the parks themselves there is absolutely no landscape, only a kitschy parody of landscaping, one which instils in the visitor the unsettling sensation of being neither quite 'inside' nor 'outside'. For a time I found it difficult to isolate the precise origin of this malaise. Then I realised that it was most intimately related to the parks' paving – seamless, unrutted, uncracked, designed not only to facilitate the movement of the crowd but, in a strange paradox, to inhume nature, to *bury the earth*. It isn't merely artificial but *cartoon* paving, with the result that, after only a hour or two, one becomes wholly unfazed by the sight of an outsized Goofy or Pluto ambling along it, one begins to feel rather like Bob Hoskins amid the cartoon creatures of *Who Framed Roger Rabbit?*

But then, what most of the parks' rides are offering visitors is precisely the opportunity to enter a movie, to dismantle the barrier of the screen, its Berlin Wall, as it were, to penetrate a spectacle of which they had always been mere spectators. In the Universal park an E. T. ride allows us if we wish not to relive but actually, vicariously, to live the film's most quintessentially Spielbergian sequences; the *Back to the Future* ride has us not simply watching Michael J. Fox travel through time in a souped-up De Lorean but ostensibly taking his place; and the faintly ghoulish *Earthquake* ride gives us a juddering inkling, *as if from the inside*, of the special effects of that now forgotten disaster movie. (Doubtless for reasons of taste and tact, no reference is made on the literature of the ride to any real, as distinct from a movie-engineered, earthquake.)

In other rides it's the film which stretches out to us instead of vice versa. This is the case with a trio of quite astounding stereoscopic exhibits: a Muppets show in which members of the furry menagerie practically curl up in one's lap; the Hitchcock exhibit in which the birds of *The Birds* take flight from the screen into the auditorium; and, in EPCOT, Coppola's weird short film *Captain EO*, with Michael Jackson and Anjelica Huston, in which Jackson's nose job looks so rubbery in three-dimensional close-up one fancies that, if one pressed it, it would pop inside-out. Never has the optical ventriloquism of 3-D 'thrown' images of such uncanny solidity and colour saturation.

A more subtle species of mental dislocation is produced by the false studio backlots of the Universal and MGM parks. Detectable here are three discrete layers of artifice: that, primarily, of the film sets themselves, since no films have ever been shot on them; a genuine film set, however, is itself an arena of illusion, often recreating a time and place long since vanished: respectively, in these parks, the New York and Hollywood of the interwar years; and the crowning illusion of all is of course that neither of these two Arcadias of populist Americana existed in anything like the paradigmatic perfection of their nostalgic theme park reproductions.

In the ideology of the theme park, then, the false is not an inferior substitute for the real, as it always used to be, but its veritable apotheosis. It purges the real of all its flaws, its injustices, its unfulfilled and unfulfillable cravings. Mercilessly eradicated are silence, boredom and rudeness: music is permanently piped through the parks (reinforcing the confusion of inside and outside); thanks to diverse audiovisual distractions, queueing up for a ride turns out to be occasionally more diverting than the ride itself; and the uniformly personable Disney staff can be relied upon for an unfailing, synthetic but not after all unsympathetic 'Have a nice day'. Ultimately, the sole blot on this Utopian landscape (or landscaping) is the indispensable but regrettably uncontrollable public, messy, noisy, unbeautiful, and overweight as only Americans can be overweight. In this incongruity if in nothing else does the theme park conform to Marianne Moore's famous definition of poetry as an imaginary garden with real toads in it.

Oh yes, it's as easy to sneer at theme parks as it is hard, after the essays of Eco (in *Travels in Hyperreality*) and the sourer, less genial Baudrillard (in his best book *Simulacra and Simulations*), to say anything very novel about them. And yet, out of all that pixilated falsity, something authentic, something gone unnoticed by either

Eco or Baudrillard, *is* generated: dare I say, happiness? It's an awkward thing to write about without condescension, but, whatever my own sense of alienation from the experience of the parks, as I strolled among the (non-semiological, non-'signreading') public, I could not help observing how amazingly *happy* everyone appeared, happy just to be there, happy to belong to a society in which Disneyland exists. I have never seen such collective, uncomplicated, lump-in-the-throat happiness, and no matter where it comes from, no matter what abuses and horrors it might be concealing, it's really rather a moving spectacle about which I find I cannot be cynical.

Frankly, when I started writing this article I had no notion that it would end on so uplifting a note, but there it is. Have a nice day.

Writers, rites and rituals

Recently the *Guardian* published its annual list of the hundred bestselling book titles of the past year. As an author myself, I was naturally concerned to see who had made it and who hadn't (while contriving to persuade myself at the same time that I wasn't still entertaining the illusion that one my own titles might miraculously have materialised on it overnight – fat chance!); to note (as a none too satisfying next best thing) how well my publisher had scored; and to deplore yet again the frightening commercial predominance of the paperback. This latter is, however, a lost cause: in times as recessionary as these, so conclusive is the case for cheaper softcover originals, for all but a golden cluster of guaranteed bestsellers, that some publishers are already gingerly predicting the hardback's imminent demise.

Would it really make a difference? For Clare Alexander at

Viking, quoted in the *Author*, the house journal of the Society of Authors, the argument for paperback 'originals' is not convincing. She does not believe that 'people who didn't want, for example, a first novel priced at £13.99 or £14.99 in hardcovers will find it irresistible at half the price'. And, replying to the same questionnaire, Felicity Rubinstein at Macmillan, while more favourably disposed to such a development, nevertheless cautions that the formula's success 'will depend upon the goodwill and co-operation of the booksellers, the press and the authors', upon their collective readiness, in short, to regard a paperback edition as other than a *reproduction* of a hardback original.

Well, notwithstanding the tenacious myth of writers as impractical dreamers, we tend on the whole to be just as sensitive to the economic realities of the business as publishers themselves are. *We want to be read* and we know that it is when incomes are no longer, as they say, disposable that books become so. Yet there is, to the experience of being published, a ceremonial quality that perhaps neither publishers nor readers are entirely capable of appreciating. To put it rather whimsically, publication is to writing what marriage is to love. It is the ritualisation (one might almost say, the sacralisation) of a passion, the transmutation of obscurity into security and a desire for posterity into a desire for (these days a very relative) prosperity. And, to extend the analogy further, being published in hardback is like being married in church whereas being published in paperback is like being married in a registrar's office. The latter is no less legitimate a formality, to be sure. Ritual, however, has been replaced by red tape, and in the absence of liturgic solemnity (that of a church ceremony or a launch party) there would seem to be an underlying implication of ephemerality, of something (a union, an edition) that is not expected to *last*.

As a writer, and I realise how pretentious this will sound, I cannot help feeling that the disappearance of such a ritual, of yet another ritual from the world, would impoverish my condition; I would even go so far as to say that I would write differently if I thought I were to be published exclusively in paperback. As a sleeper's dreams may be subtly revised by an ache in his shoulder or a crease in his pillow, so everything that is contingent on and contiguous to the act of writing, from the clutter of one's desk to the angle of one's anglepoise lamp, may influence what it is that one writes.

Consider simply what one writes *with* or *on*. Successively, over the years, I have had recourse to a pencil, a pen, a manual typewriter, an electric typewriter, a basic Amstrad computer and, currently, an Apple Macintosh, that veritable Amstradivarius of word processors. Not only has each of these different supports altered what and how I have written, for better or worse, but I would also claim to be able to tell, from the sole internal evidence of the text, with which type of instrument another writer has written his or her book.

To demonstrate how I would distinguish, first, between typed and handwritten texts (they still exist), let me draw another, on this occasion musical, analogy. If typing a text is like playing the piano, then handwriting it can be compared to playing the violin: the 'style' of the first support is percussive and discontinuous while that of the second tends to be much more fluid, meandering and lyrical. (In this light it's worth noting that an error in handwriting resembles a mistake on the violin: the 'note' simply doesn't exist; whereas a typewritten error resembles one played on the piano: the note may be wrong but it's nevertheless recognisably a note.) As for a word processor, because all of its erasures are instantly expunged, instantly invisible, it grants the writer easy access to a syntactical complexity from which he or she would probably, unconsciously, recoil if it were to result in the unsightly scorings-out of a handwritten page or the equally unsightly xxxxxxxxxxs, those little kisses-to-make-it-better, on a typewritten page.

It's inconceivable, then, that a skyscraper of a novel like *The Runaway Soul* or *Foucault's Pendulum* could have been produced on anything else but a computer (the former mimicking the handwritten mode, as computers enable one to do, the latter blissfully revelling in its cybernetic delirium). Inconceivable, too, that Martin Amis could have calculated the retroverted morbidities of *Time's Arrow* on a mere typewriter. Inconceivable, finally, that the sort of 'shopping and chopping' fiction exemplified by Bret Easton Ellis's *American Psycho* (if Easton Ellis were ever to rewrite the *Odyssey* – bear with me, please – he would doubtless refer to 'the Beaujolais Nouveau-dark sea') did not first see the light of day on a computer screen. Some things are just too crass to have been written by hand.

Van Gogh

Van Gogh. It was in 1989, just a couple of years short of the centenary of the artist's death, that these two words became, as one observer put it, 'an index of art market buoyancy in the face of stock market decline'. In March of that year one of Van Gogh's several sunflower paintings went for £24,750,000; in June *The Bridge at Trinquetaille* fetched £12,650,000; and November saw the sale of his *Irises* in New York for a record-breaking figure of £27,450,000. So intense was the publicity surrounding the last of these sales that Sotheby's actually, and in its history surely uniquely, published an expensive catalogue devoted to the single item up for auction. In a world in which a painting's market value has now come to replace the painter's signature as the philistine measure of his genius, it would not be too fanciful to claim that Vincent Van Gogh is the most famous painter of all time.

There was, however, another, very much less publicised, record that Van Gogh was breaking at the same time: no artist in any medium has been as frequently portrayed in the cinema. Back in 1956, of course, Kirk Douglas played him in Vincente Minnelli's

Lust For Life. But of late there have been no fewer than four screen Van Goghs: John Hurt in Paul Cox's *Vincent*, Tim Roth in Robert Altman's *Vincent & Theo*, the filmmaker Martin Scorsese, of all improbable casting coups, in an indescribably garish episode of Kurosawa's *Dreams* and Jacques Dutronc, a French pop singer and occasional actor, in Maurice Pialat's three-hour *Van Gogh*, the latest and by far the most persuasive portrait of all.

In each of these films the paintings themselves (and those which we are given to see are invariably those most familiar to us already) are naturally identical, perfect copies of famous originals. Yet, like those odd individuals who never seem to photograph the same way twice, not one of the various Van Goghs who are supposed to have painted them actually looks, sounds or even holds his brush like any of his rivals. Which is perhaps the property of every myth: as long as its fundamental parameters are respected, as long as that cluster of emblematic singularities by which it becomes instantly recognisable remains inviolate, it can withstand virtually any tinkering and manhandling.

For think of a few other painters whose lives have also been filmed: most famously, Toulouse-Lautrec (in John Huston's *Moulin Rouge*), Michelangelo (in Carol Reed's *The Agony and the Ecstasy*), Gauguin (in Albert Lewin's *The Moon and Sixpence*), Modigliani (in Jacques Becker's *Montparnasse 19*), Caravaggio (in Derek Jarman's *Caravaggio*) and Rembrandt (in Alexander Korda's *Rembrandt*).

In each instance the director has elected to focus on the painter's mythical distinguishing feature, the most piquant and showy fetish-image of his personal iconography, the most obvious 'hook' or 'angle' of his life – in short, the single fact about him with which audiences are likely to be conversant even before they enter the cinema. It might be Lautrec's two dwarflike stumps (the artist as freak), Michelangelo's Sistine Chapel ceiling (the artist as demiurge), Gauguin's sultry Tahitian mistresses (the artist as lotus-eater), Modigliani's absinthe-soaked café trawl (the artist as Bohemian), Caravaggio's low-life intimacy with prostitutes, thieves and homosexuals (the artist as outcast) or Rembrandt's tireless self-portraiture (the artist as scrutiniser of the soul).

There can be little doubt that it was those angles rather than the quality of the painters' work that got the movies made in the first place. And the deeply satisfying thing about Van Gogh, from the filmmaker's point of view at least, is that all of these ingredients are combined in one person. Thus, since the single fact about him of which everyone is aware is that, in a fit of dementia, he sliced off his ear (more accurately, a small part of the lobe), he too was something of a freak, that missing ear, literally *conspicuous by its absence*, constituting a marvellous, albeit invisible, prop for the more flamboyant type of character actor. His canvases were often as thickly applied and variegated as palettes, which lent him the demiurgic aura of an action painter *avant la lettre*, a nineteenth-century Jackson Pollock. Although of course Dutch, and briefly resident in France's sunlessly grim industrial north, popular tradition more commonly associates him with its southern regions, which adds the requisite touch of Gauguinesque sybaritism; and, no less a connoisseur of absinthe than Modigliani, his Bohemian credentials are at least as unimpeachable. His insanity, anti-social attitudes and confrontational manner also made him an outcast, as did the fact that he only ever sold one painting in his own lifetime – like Mozart he resembled one of those tramps of ubiquitous folk myth who die in poverty and are revealed after their deaths to be millionaires. As for soul-scrutinising, he painted as many as forty-three self-portraits, in all of which were prominent the probing eyes, high-boned skull, coarse red beard and tortured proto-Expressionist brush-strokes (almost as though his personality were so intense it had started to emit vibrations) which have caused him to become one of the most easily identified of great artists.

Not just easily identified, moreover, but easily mimicked, easily fictionalised. Because Van Gogh painted exclusively from nature, and eschewed religious and historical subject-matter, he bequeathed intact to posterity a readily adaptable visual iconography, even a handy cast of picturesque supporting characters and walk-ons – his friend Gauguin, Doctor Gachet, the poet Boch, the postman Roulin – of which filmmakers in particular have seen no reason not to take generous advantage. He also personified the evergreen Romantic theme of the alienation, professional and psychic, of an artist from a society indifferent to his genius, and offered through his correspondence with his brother Theo, a glimpse into the mindset of one of the most heroic individualists of the nineteenth century.

With all that, his was what the movies love best, a success story – if only posthumously, at Sotheby's, almost a century after his death. Like a fairy-tale Prince, he died and lived happily ever after.

Benetton and God

How would one 'sell' God? By which I mean, were God to take it into His head to retain a public relations firm, some celestial Saatchi & Saatchi, to burnish an image that He suspected had lost a lot of its lustre, on precisely what angles would its copywriters be advised to focus?

Well, in view of the currently calamitous state of His creation, they would probably judge it politic to play down the conventional divine attributes of love, justice, mercy and wisdom and instead draw attention to such less contentious qualities as His benign and diffuse omnipresence, His unfailing patience, His sheer universality. Thus they might launch the campaign with a series of billboard posters on which faces representing every race, colour and creed, as they say, were seen to coexist in the naïve and Edenic harmony of those 'peaceable kingdom' tableaux that one remembers from childhood albums; and if these faces were themselves to be of children, what could be more appropriate and fetching?

Yet it would be essential to make the point that God's universality is not merely geographical but metaphysical in nature, to recall to the potential client His enduring immanence at the great elemental epiphanies of human experience. For this a more sophisticated style of campaigning would have to be envisaged, with a spread of stark, startling, uncaptioned photographs, perhaps, designed to evoke a few of the more critical conjunctures of life and death: a newborn babe, a young man dying of Aids, a guerrilla fighter brandishing a human bone.

In short, and the reader no doubt already knows what I'm going to say next, one would sell God exactly as Benetton sells jumpers.

The problem is that, aside from the fact that both God and Benetton work in mysterious ways, and that their respective products have to be taken on faith (and, speaking personally, my belief in the existence of God is quite a lot stronger than my belief in the quality of a Benetton jumper), it's by no means easy at first to discern what it is that they might have in common: or, putting it another way, to understand how an advertising campaign befitting the promotion of God could also be used to promote knitwear. What is it, beyond its own brand name, that Benetton is attempting to sell? The answer, surely, is the universality that I have already mentioned.

Now, that may seem a ludicrously overweening ambition to ascribe to a mere fashion retailer. Yet Coca-Cola, to consider only the most emblematic case in point, is in strict geographical terms more literally 'universal' than at least the Judaeo-Christian God and for many years now its advertising has been calculated more to remind us of its existence than to persuade us of its excellence. It has ceased in a sense to be a cultural and become virtually a natural phenomenon. For the demographically 'average' child (which is to say, a child of the working, lower-middle or middle class, the sort whose earliest formative experience is of *shopping*, of being wheeled along supermarket lanes in a pushchair, like a good little consumer in embryo) a Coca-Cola can is a more familiar artefact than a tulip. And if Benetton can hardly claim the same household-name familiarity, it seems likely that its present campaign is meant to short-circuit the process, to propel it into the exclusive club of manufacturers whose products' names have 'entered the language', to insinuate the notion, subliminally if need be, that, while it may be humanity's lot to be born, fall ill and die, Benetton remains immutable, indestructible, incorruptible. Benetton, in other words, just *is*.

The peculiar beauty of the scheme, from the company's own point of view, is that it's not just the product but the very promotion of that product, and the controversy surrounding it, which ends by being publicised. An attention-seizing double-page blank spread in *Elle*, instead of the photograph of the Aids sufferer which the company's deliberate delaying tactics forced the magazine's editor to make an eleventh-hour decision to pull, only shrieks Benetton at us the more clamorously. And this article of mine cannot avoid becoming an advertisement for it in its turn.

The photograph in question is actually a very beautiful one, by the power with which it demonstrates yet again how, in moments of extreme distress (the young man had apparently no more than a few instants left of his life to live), ordinary people instinctively contrive to adopt postures as eloquent as those devised by the greatest painters, and it's naturally a trifle disheartening to learn that the victim's family gave (or else sold) permission for Benetton to exploit it. Morally, if not legally, however, the only permission that mattered, the only authority that could ever have sanctioned such exploitation, was that of the young man himself, whose consent was obviously neither sought nor obtained.

The whole exercise, then, is not just an insult to the public's intelligence but simply, unambiguously immoral, and for once there would appear to be nothing to prevent one from acting upon one's disgust: in view of their completely unexceptional nature, Benetton's jumpers are easily boycottable. And I cannot help thinking of the hero of another recent advertising campaign, sweet old J. R. Hartley, and of his namesake L. P., who famously wrote in *The Go-Between*: 'The past is a foreign country. They do things differently there.' As a rule, it gives me no pleasure to be seen striking a fogeyish attitude, but when I see what is currently judged permissible in the sacred name of salesmanship, I sometimes wonder whether it isn't rather the present that is the foreign country, and here and now that things are being done differently.

Capital letters

Words are weird things, letters too sometimes. Or perhaps it's simple professional deformation on my part, the fact that I spend most of my working life staring at the damn things, that encourages me to find them so versatile and volatile. I can never see the expression 'holier-than-thou', for example, without mentally capitalising it as 'Holier-than-Thou', whom I imagine to be an especially sanctimonious Vietnamese monk; another common expression, 'remains to be seen', infallibly makes me think of Greece and the Parthenon; and, letter-wise, I particularly cherish the aptness of that plunging 'V' in the word 'Valley' in contrast to the properly Alpine serration of the 'M' of 'Mountains'. More generally, though, I have often wondered how many letters have to be altered in a word before it ceases altogether to be recognisable.

Take the word 'London'. It can still be identified in 'Londop', and just about in 'Landop', but when one arrives at 'Handop', let's say, the city has completely disappeared. 'London' is a shortish word, it's true, but it's remarkable how very few such substitutions are required for the nature of even more extended words to be transformed out of all recognition.

Imagine, now, the word 'London' as a hypersimplified ideogram of the capital's skyline. The 'L' would be Big Ben, the first 'o' the dome of St Paul's Cathedral, the first 'n' Marble Arch, the 'd' Westminster Abbey, the second 'o' the dome of the Albert Hall and the second 'n' Tower Bridge. And the question is: How many of these landmarks could be removed from the city before it itself ceased to be what we think of as 'London'?

As in any febrile pre-election period, the capital's future is once more on the agenda (on Labour's agenda at least), as witness the publication of the manifesto *A New London* by the architect Richard Rogers and the Shadow Minister for the Arts, Mark Fisher. As its authors acknowledge, any refurbishment of the capital which hopes to be both radical and humane will have to reconcile numerous and frequently contradictory imperatives, from the redevelopment of London's depressed inner city areas to the maintenance of its role as the financial centre of Europe – matters which I, a total layman, am more or less content to leave to the much-vilified experts. At the same time, as just one of the city's many long-suffering inhabitants, I find myself tempted to offer a revolutionary if also selfish and whimsical counter-proposal. *Leave the bloody thing alone!*

It is because of decades of interventionist urban planning that London is now, frankly, the ugliest and tattiest capital in Europe. London is equally, however, to revert to the linguistic analogy, a living, ancient *text*, one which has been subject over the years to multiple erasures and revisions, to the capricious and not always consistent addition and subtraction of subordinate clauses, and one major preoccupation of the planners surely ought to be just how much of it can be altered again before it has quite lost its messy, tentacular and oddly mysterious character.

There is, of course, no chance that any of the edifices listed above will one day actually disappear. But London Bridge, after all, has been transplanted to Texas, Battersea Power Station squats gutted and idle, Piccadilly Circus ('the hub of the universe' in the Englishman's preposterously Ptolemeian vision of the world) is a travesty of what it used to be and Downing Street has become, and under John Major seems fated to remain, a fenced-in enclave. More significantly if less conspicuously, every day sees the demolition of a building that, no matter how ungainly it might have been in and of itself, was once an integral element in a coherent cityscape. Did they all really have to come down? Or could some of them fairly be compared to bad teeth which might have been saved with a little preventive care, instead of being replaced, as most have been, by the horrible grinning dentures of impersonal and not even particularly lofty skyscrapers?

That London is not Venice or Paris or Toledo, that it is not one of those beautiful and faintly museumlike cities that no one would dare to improve upon, paradoxically renders it all the more fragile and vulnerable. The fact, too, that once the process is under way there is potentially no end to the construction and reconstruction that demands to be undertaken, with unsightly scaffolding removed from one façade only and instantly to be raised on to another, means that the city is fated to remain in a condition of permanent repair and ruin (for nothing more resembles a half-erected building than one in an advanced state of dilapidation) – its galleries obscured by the metallic cross-hatching of scaffolding, its museums swathed in rust-cankered cobwebs, its hospitals propped up on massive tubular crutches, its colleges choked by the gangrenous ivy of green tarpaulin, its boutiques patched up like old pairs of corduroy jeans. So why not just let it be?

It won't happen, I know. The humourist George S. Kaufman, a New Yorker obsessed for most of his professional life with the din and dust of construction sites – construction sites, he began to suspect, erected for the exclusive purpose of plaguing his days and haunting his nights ('Let's *get* Kaufman,' he imagined the word being passed from hard-hat to hard-hat across the city at 7am) – wrote somewhere of a marvellous dream that he had had. In it he dreamt of waking up one morning with a start. Instead of the unholy pandaemonium which had regularly shattered his sleep there was an eerie, inexplicable silence. He scrambled out of bed, hustled on some clothes and dashed down into the street. What he saw there, as he told the tale, were construction workers all over the city packing up their tools, unscrewing their scaffolding and driving away in their steamrollers, cement-mixers and tip-up trucks. Consumed with curiosity, he accosted one of them and asked what was going on.

'We're finished,' was the reply.

'Finished?' echoed the mystified Kaufman.

'Yeah,' the hard-hat continued, 'We're goin' home now. New York's finished.'

A dream, as I say.

Flash trash

A recent issue of *Esquire* carried the first of what seemed to be intended as a monthly glossary of, I quote, 'useful words for the nineties'. The word selected to launch this glossary was 'flash', which the magazine defined as 'no longer pejorative, but denoting flamboyance, daring and a propensity for taking risks in one's chosen field'. And that definition was illustrated by a cluster of the decade's sociocultural cynosures: flash novelists (Tom Wolfe, Martin Amis, Don DeLillo), flash politicians (Tony Banks, Michael Heseltine, Paul Boateng), flash actors (Gary Oldman, John Malkovich, Tim Roth), flash artists (Jeff Koons, Damien Hirst, Martin Kippenberger), flash couturiers (Gianni Versace, Claude Montana, Thierry Mugler), and so on.

It's true enough that in certain fashionable or, shall we say, 'flashionable' quarters the term has indeed shed its once derogatory connotations, even though it's possible to argue that relatively few of these flash notables, whatever their individual gifts, are likely to possess any longer-term powers of creative durability: in this context 'flash' may well turn out to be short for 'flash-in-the-pan'. But what I would like to counter-propose is another, increasingly prevalent cultural category of the nineties, in this case an unequivocally negative one: Flash Trash.

Flash Trash is what is produced when artistic modes that used to be regarded as irreconcilably incompatible with one another – the experimental and the exploitative, the enduring and the ephemeral, etc. – are conflated in a calculated attempt to dupe the (mostly youthful) consumer. Sheltering under the gaudy catch-all parasol of the postmodern, or what journalistically passes for postmodernism, Flash Trash deploys the strategies of high art to camouflage codes and practices that were once the sole preserve of potboiling hacks and has thus contrived to generate a whole new series of cultural oxymorons: synthetic authenticity, expensive cheapness, glossy sleaze. It is a form of the Midas myth in which whatever the artist touches is transformed into not gold but glitz. It is, to put it crudely, shit polished up until it glows and gleams (except that the smell can never quite be removed).

As an envious – indeed, frankly jealous – admirer of his earlier fictions, it saddens me to have to say this, but Nicholson Baker's *Vox*, for example, is a choice specimen of Flash Trash. No matter how unexpectedly accessible the result, the extreme centripetality, verging on provocation, of Baker's first, reputation-making book *The Mezzanine*, whose narrative was entirely constructed around the lunch-break purchase of a sandwich and a shoelace, was a genuine leap into virginal territory, a prime number, as mathematicians say. No less *sui generis* was *U & I*, about its author's faintly phantasmagoric relationship with John Updike, an amazing portrait of the artist as a brilliant, mean-minded wimp. Neither of these works represented an obvious commercial calculation, neither was what might be called a marketing coup, both of them were indisputably labours of love. But *Vox*, whether consciously or not, is a calculation on Baker's part, a cast-iron contract drawn up between him, his publisher and his readers, a sex-and-literature package in which absolutely nothing has been left to chance. (Even the monosyllabically neutral title is upstaged on the book's cover by an explicit subtitle, 'A Novel about Telephone Sex', designed to leave no casual, impulsive bookshop browser in the dark as to the precise nature of the juicy goodies within its pages.) It is, in short, a book whose specific and perhaps even sole goal was to propel Baker out of the ungrateful realm of the *succès d'estime* and into that of the *succès de scandale*.

Exemplifying current Flash Trash in the cinema are Martin Scorsese's *Cape Fear* and Barry Levinson's *Bugsy*. Now, it may seem churlish and ungrateful to reject out of hand two such grand splashy entertainments, especially from filmmakers who have done good work in the past. But the brutish misogyny of the former and the latter's preposterous attempt to portray a big dumb racketeer as some kind of raffish visionary (his vision is Las Vegas!) serve to demonstrate that their creators, however talented they might once have been, are no longer *free men*, have become slaves, not to put too fine a point on it, to the most blatant and crass of commercial ideologies. (It might be worth adding that the phenomenon is by no means exclusively based in Hollywood or exclusively fuelled by budgetary considerations. Lars von Trier's *Europa*, an inexpensive European 'art movie', is filmic Flash Trash of a particularly repellent, Nazi-haunted type.)

The thing is everywhere now. Peter Hall's TV adaptation of Mary Wesley's *The Camomile Lawn* is sexy-genteel Flash Trash of a peculiarly British cast. Once so witty and bracing, the prose of Gore Vidal's essays has, in *A View from the Diners Club*, grown smug, narcissistic and jowly – belletristic Flash Trash. (Vidal, whose literary career has described a downward spiral exactly parallel to that of the homosexual French novelist and scandalmonger Roger Peyrefitte, ritually grouches that the allure of the cinema has eclipsed that of the novel for all but academics: well, but who wouldn't rather see practically any movie than plough through the Michheneresque thickets of his own *Creation* or *Hollywood*?) The recent Party Election Broadcasts of Hugh Hudson and John Schlesinger constitute political Flash Trash – more precisely, the first was undiluted flash, the second undiluted trash. And so it goes.

However influential have been the many and various theoretical pieties to which the arts have been invited to pay lip service over the years, the artist's sacred duty has remained the same since Cyril Connolly once defined it categorically as being 'to produce a masterpiece'. But if most of the names I have cited are or have been artists, they have now apparently chosen to forget that a work of art can never be created in accordance with a calculation or a contract or a Faustian pact sealed with the flashiest and most superficial trappings of the cultural zeitgeist. An authentic work of art, let alone a masterpiece, is always conceived, as it were, out of wedlock. A natural child, a love child.

Index